# Third Workshop on Spatial Language Understanding (SpLU 2020)



Online
19 November 2020

ISBN: 978-1-7138-2004-8

**Printed from e-media with permission by:**

Curran Associates, Inc.
57 Morehouse Lane
Red Hook, NY 12571

**Some format issues inherent in the e-media version may also appear in this print version.**



Printed with permission by Curran Associates, Inc. (2021)

For permission requests, please contact the Association for Computational Linguistics at the address below.

Association for Computational Linguistics
209 N. Eighth Street
Stroudsburg, Pennsylvania 18360

Phone: 1-570-476-8006
Fax: 1-570-476-0860

acl@aclweb.org

**Additional copies of this publication are available from:**

Curran Associates, Inc.
57 Morehouse Lane
Red Hook, NY 12571 USA
Phone: 845-758-0400
Fax: 845-758-2633
Email: curran@proceedings.com
Web: www.proceedings.com

EMNLP 2020

# Spatial Language Understanding
# (SpLU 2020)

## Proceedings of the Third Workshop

November 19, 2020

# Introduction

Welcome to the Third International Workshop on Spatial Language Understanding (SpLU 2020). The goal of this workshop is to bring together researchers working on computational models for spatial language understanding from different perspectives including cognitive linguistic studies and spatial information representations for machine learning and reasoning. Spatial semantics of the language is important in many real-world language understanding and language generation applications which makes it worth special attention. Examples of such applications are human-machine interaction and grounded dialogue systems, geographical information systems, systems that need combining vision and language such as visual question answering, navigation, and instruction-following agents. Since spatial semantics is related to the physical world, it can be visualized (except for the metaphoric usage). Thus, such semantics are important to be explored for text-to-scene conversion and vice-versa, that is, for text/caption generation for visual information such as images and videos. For this workshop, we called for research papers on spatial language meaning representations (continuous, symbolic), corpus collection and analysis, learning to extract spatial information, reasoning based on spatial language, spatial language grounding, and combining vision and language, and applications of spatial language in various downstream tasks.

This year, we received 13 submissions directly to the workshop (10 in the archival track and 3 in the non-archival track). After a rigorous review process, we accepted 7 submissions in the archival track and 3 in the nonarchival track. Moreover, based on the ACL new policies and the new Findings papers track, 11 papers from Findings were directed to the SpLU workshop from which we accepted 8 papers based on their relevance to the theme of the workshop. This volume is dedicated to the 7 papers from the archival track. The main contributions from the accepted papers in all the tracks (archival, non-archival, and Findings) range from all of the aforementioned topics. The workshop includes papers on cognitively motivated approaches as well as deep learning language models for spatial information extraction and location recognition, spatial question answering, navigation and grounding, instruction following and assembly tasks, and even applications of spatial information extraction in the medical domain and patient reports. It covers, data collection, introducing new corpora, annotation scheme and datasets, spatial information in Dialogue systems, and generating scenes based on spatial descriptions. The topics cover exciting research works that highlight the current efforts, challenges, and future endeavors for spatial language understanding research.

We thank our programming committee members, invited speakers, and authors, without whose help and contributions, this workshop would not have been possible. We look forward to seeing you virtually on November 19, 2020.

**Organizers:**

Parisa Kordjamshidi, Michigan State University
Archna Bhatia, Institute for Human and Machine Cognition
Malihe Alikhani, University of Pittsburgh
Jason Baldridge, Google
Mohit Bansal, UNC Chapel Hill
Marie-Francine Moens, KU Leuven

**Program Committee:**

Steven Bethard, The University of Arizona (USA)
Raffaella Bernardi, University of Trento (Italy)
Mehul Bhatt, Örebro University - CoDesign Lab (Sweden)
Yonatan Bisk, Carnegie Mellon University (USA)
Johan Bos, University of Groningen (The Netherlands)
Asli Celikyilmaz, Microsoft Research (USA)
Joyce Chai, University of Michigan (USA)
Angel Xuan Chang, Simon Fraser University (Canada)
Anthony Cohn, University of Leeds (England)
Guillem Collell, KU Leuven (Belgium)
Simon Dobnik, University of Gothenburg (Sweden)
Bonnie J. Dorr, Institute for Human and Machine Cognition (USA)
Ekaterina Egorova, University of Zurich (Switzerland)
Zoe Falomir, Universitat Bremen (Germany)
Francis Ferraro, University of Maryland Baltimore (USA)
Lucian Galescu, Institute for Human and Machine Cognition (USA)
Mehdi Ghanimifard, University of Gothenburg (Sweden)
Julia Hockenmaier, University of Illinois at Urbana-Champaign (USA)
Lei Li, Bytedance (China)
Bruno Martins, University of Lisbon (Portugal)
Srini Narayanan, Google Inc. (USA)
Mari Broman Olsen, Lionbridge AI (USA)
Martijn van Otterlo, Open University (The Netherlands)
Ian Perera, Institute for Human and Machine Cognition (USA)
Kirk Roberts, UT Health (USA)
Manolis Savva, Stanford University (USA)
Kristin Stock, Massey University (New Zealand)
Jesse Thomason, University of Washington (USA)
Clare Voss, ARL (USA)

**Invited Speaker:**

Yoav Artzi, Cornell University
Bonnie Dorr, Institute for Human and Machine Cognition
Julia Hockenmaier, University of Illinois at Urbana-Champaign
Douwe Kiela, Facebook
James Pustejovsky, Brandeis University

# Table of Contents

# Workshop Program

**Thursday, November 19, 2020**

**8:00–9:00** **GatherTown I**

**9:00–10:48** **Session 1**
**9:00–9:10** ***Opening Talk***
**9:10–10:00** ***Invited talk: James Pustejovsky***
**10:00–10:56** ***Paper Presentations (SpLU, Findings)***
10:00–10:14 *An Element-wise Visual-enhanced BiLSTM-CRF Model for Location Name Recognition*
Takuya Komada and Takashi Inui
10:14–10:28 *BERT-based Spatial Information Extraction*
Hyeong Jin Shin, Jeong Yeon Park, Dae Bum Yuk and Jae Sung Lee
10:28–10:42 *A Cognitively Motivated Approach to Spatial Information Extraction*
Chao Xu, Emmanuelle-Anna Dietz Saldanha, Dagmar Gromann and Beihai Zhou
10:42–10:56 *Language-Conditioned Feature Pyramids for Visual Selection Tasks (Findings)*
Taichi Iki and Akiko Aizawa

10:56–11:05 *Break*

**11:05–12:51** **Session 2**
**11:05–11:55** ***Invited talk: Julia Hockenmeier***
**11:55–12:51** ***Paper Presentations (SpLU, Findings)***
11:55–12:09 *They are not all alike: answering different spatial questions requires different grounding strategies*
Alberto Testoni, Claudio Greco, Tobias Bianchi, Mauricio Mazuecos, Agata Marcante, Luciana Benotti and Raffaella Bernardi
12:09–12:23 *Categorisation, Typicality & Object-Specific Features in Spatial Referring Expressions*
Adam Richard-Bollans, Anthony Cohn and Lucía Gómez Álvarez
12:23–12:37 *A Linguistic Analysis of Visually Grounded Dialogues Based on Spatial Expressions (Findings)*
Takuma Udagawa, Takato Yamazaki and Akiko Aizawa
12:37–12:51 *Visually-Grounded Planning without Vision: Language Models Infer Detailed Plans from High-level Instructions (Findings)*
Peter A. Jansen

12:51–13:00 *Break*

**13:00–14:46** **Session 3**
**13:00–13:50** ***Invited talk: Yoav Artzi***
**13:50–14:46** ***Paper Presentations (SpLU, Findings)***
13:50–14:04 *A Hybrid Deep Learning Approach for Spatial Trigger Extraction from Radiology Reports*
Surabhi Datta and Kirk Roberts
14:04–14:18 *Retouchdown: Releasing Touchdown on StreetLearn as a Public Resource for Language Grounding Tasks in Street View*
Harsh Mehta, Yoav Artzi, Jason Baldridge, Eugene Ie and Piotr Mirowski

**Thursday, November 19, 2020 (continued)**

14:18–14:32 *SpaRTQA: A Textual Question Answering Benchmark for Spatial Reasoning (Non-archival)*
Roshanak Mirzaee, Hossein Rajaby Faghihi and Parisa Kordjamshidi

14:32–14:46 *Decoding Language Spatial Relations to 2D Spatial Arrangements (Findings)*
Gorjan Radevski, Guillem Collell, Marie-Francine Moens and Tinne Tuytelaars

14:46–15:45 *Break*

**15:45–17:31 Session 4**

**15:45–16:35 *Invited talk: Bonnie Dorr***

**16:35–17:31 *Paper Presentations (SpLU, Findings)***

16:35–16:49 *Geocoding with multi-level loss for spatial language representation (Non-archival)*
Sayali Kulkarni, Shailee Jain, Mohammad Javad Hosseini, Jason Baldridge, Eugene Ie and Li Zhang

16:49–17:03 *Vision-and-Language Navigation by Reasoning over Spatial Configurations (Non-archival)*
Yue Zhang, Quan Guo and Parisa Kordjamshidi

17:03–17:17 *LiMiT: The Literal Motion in Text Dataset (Findings)*
Irene Manotas, Ngoc Phuoc An Vo and Vadim Sheinin

17:17–17:31 *ARRAMON: A Joint Navigation-Assembly Instruction Interpretation Task in Dynamic Environments (Findings)*
Hyounghun Kim, Abhay Zala, Graham Burri, Hao Tan and Mohit Bansal

17:31–17:45 *Break*

**17:45–19:00 Session 5**

**17:45–18:35 *Invited talk: Douwe Kiela***

**18:35–19:00 *Paper Presentations (Findings)***

18:35–18:49 *Robust and Interpretable Grounding of Spatial References with Relation Networks (Findings)*
Tsung-Yen Yang, Andrew S. Lan and Karthik Narasimhan

18:49–19:03 *RMM: A Recursive Mental Model for Dialogue Navigation (Findings)*
Homero Roman Roman, Yonatan Bisk, Jesse Thomason, Asli Celikyilmaz and Jianfeng Gao

**19:03–20:00 Panel Discussion**

**20:00–21:00 GatherTown II**

# An Element-wise Visual-enhanced BiLSTM-CRF Model for Location Name Recognition

**Takuya Komada**
Department of Computer Science
University of Tsukuba
komada@mibel.cs.tsukuba.ac.jp

**Takashi Inui**
Department of Computer Science
University of Tsukuba
inui@cs.tsukuba.ac.jp

## Abstract

In recent years, previous studies have used visual information in named entity recognition (NER) for social media posts with attached images. However, these methods can only be applied to documents with attached images. In this paper, we propose a NER method that can use element-wise visual information for any documents by using image data corresponding to each word in the document. The proposed method obtains element-wise image data using an image retrieval engine, to be used as extra features in the neural NER model. Experimental results on the standard Japanese NER dataset show that the proposed method achieves a higher F1 value (89.67%) than a baseline method in location name recognition, demonstrating the effectiveness of using element-wise visual information.

Figure 1: Images of urban cities: (left) Shenzhen, China, (right) Dubai, UAE.

Figure 2: Images of rural villages: (left) Manali, India, (right) Hakone, Japan.

## 1 Introduction

Since the 1990s, information extraction, in which computers are used to extract structured data from unstructured documents, has been extensively studied (Cowie and Lehnert, 1996; Grishman and Sundheim, 1996). Among the entities to be extracted, location information (where) is one of the essential components (5W1H) of event information to be extracted, and the process has evolved to include various tasks, such as location name disambiguation and mapping of location names to real-world geographic locations (Weissenbacher et al., 2019).

Location name recognition has been typically conducted as a named entity recognition (NER) task (Li et al., 2018). In this field, deep learning models using visual information have been actively studied in recent years, especially in the extraction of named entities (NEs) from posts in social networking services (SNSs) such as Twitter and SnapChat (Lu et al., 2018; Moon et al., 2019; Zhang et al., 2018). These methods use images attached to a post as multimodal features to disambiguate word meanings in the post. For example, the word *Washington* can be used to refer to Washington, D.C. (LOCATION) or the presidency of George Washington (PERSON). Looking at the attached image, *Washington* could be further disambiguated.

As mentioned above, visual information is considered capable of explaining word meanings and provide useful information for location name recognition. For example, Figure 1 shows images of two different modernized cities, Shenzhen in China and Dubai in the UAE, and Figure 2 shows images of rural villages, Manali in India and Hakone in Japan. One can easily recognize common objects from these images: skyscrapers in Figure 1, and townscapes surrounded by mountains and rivers in Figure 2. Similarities like these would provide sufficient information to consider that words like *Shenzhen* and *Dubai* in documents have the same NE aspect.



*Proceedings of the Third International Workshop on Spatial Language Understanding (SpLU 2020)*, pages 1–9
November 19, 2020. 
https://doi.org/10.18653/v1/P17

In this paper, we propose a method for location name recognition that utilizes images more effectively. Specifically, image data are obtained for each word in a document through an image retrieval engine, using the words in the document as a search query, and used as an extra multimodal feature in a neural NER model. The proposed model has two advantages. First, it is robust to unseen words that do not appear in the training data; standard NER models tend to be vulnerable to unseen words. Image data corresponding to each word in the document would provide additional information to clarify word meanings, as shown in the examples of Figure 1 and Figure 2. Second, our method can be applied to any documents to obtain element-wise image data corresponding to each word in the document; those of previous studies can only be applied to documents with images attached to them.

In addition, in the proposed method, we introduce a Gate mechanism to control the extent to which the visual features from images are input to the neural NER model. Polysemous words, abbreviations, and misspellings in a document could result in inappropriate instances in the image data obtained by the image retrieval engine. The gate's function is to remove the harmful effects derived from these instances by increasing or decreasing the degree of effect of a visual feature in the model when an image is appropriate or inappropriate for the document's context, respectively.

We evaluate the model's performance for location name recognition using a standard BiLSTM-CRF model as our baseline and then show the effectiveness of element-wise visual information and Gate mechanism, through our experimental results.

## 2 Related Work

### 2.1 Neural NER Model

In NER, machine learning models using conditional random fields (CRFs) have been widely used (Marcińczuk, 2015). Since the emergence of deep learning in recent years, it has become common to use various neural network-based NER models. Among them, bidirectional long short-term memory (LSTM) models that include a CRF layer, BiLSTM-CRF, are one of the most common models (Huang et al., 2015; Lample et al., 2016). Furthermore, a variation of BiLSTM-CRF with pre-trained language models for large unsupervised corpora such as Flair (Akbik et al., 2018) have been successful in achieving high performance.

### 2.2 Use of Visual Information

Visual information obtained from images (or pictures) has been used in neural NER models, especially when applied to SNS posts that include images related to them. Moon et al. (2019) proposed a neural NER model using images attached to a post as multimodal features. In the model, the image is transformed into a vector representation through a pre-trained CNN-based image recognition model and then combined with the input to the LSTM network for NER. Asgari-Chenaghlu et al. (2020) proposed a similar model to Moon et al. (2019) that could directly use object name class labels obtained by the image recognition model. Lu et al. (2018) and Zhang et al. (2018) proposed models that obtain one-to-one correspondences between a word in a document and an object in a picture attached to the document to obtain fine-grained visual features. These studies only use image data attached to the document, not element-wise image data corresponding to words in the document.

In Chinese NER, each part of a Chinese character in a document can be regarded as a visual feature and mixed into the NER model (Jia and Ma, 2019). Although this model handles element-wise visual information in the same manner as ours, that is, image data corresponding to each element (character or word) in the document are used in the NER model, it only focuses on the characters' patterns. Our model, described in detail in Section 4, focuses on images that express word meanings.

## 3 BiLSTM-CRF Model

This section describes the details of the BiLSTM-CRF model as a basis for our baseline model. As mentioned in the previous section, the BiLSTM-CRF model is one of the most common models for NER. The input is a word or character sequence in a document and the output is a sequence of labels representing NE information. In this study, we use a character-based model because the dataset used in the experiments is Japanese and errors caused by word segmentation can be ignored. Character-based models have been confirmed to outperform word-based models when Japanese documents are used (Misawa et al., 2017).

Let $\boldsymbol{C} = \{c_t\}_{t=1}^{M}$ be the input character sequence, $\boldsymbol{x} = \{\boldsymbol{x}_t\}_{t=1}^{M}$ be the input vector sequence corresponding to $\boldsymbol{C}$, and $\boldsymbol{y} = \{y_t\}_{t=1}^{M}$ be the output label sequence. Here, $\boldsymbol{x}$ is created by concatenating three types of vector (embedding) sequences $\boldsymbol{x}_c$, $\boldsymbol{x}_w$, and $\boldsymbol{x}_F$. The $t$-th element $\boldsymbol{x}_t$ of $\boldsymbol{x}$ is given by Equation (1).

$$\boldsymbol{x}_t = [\boldsymbol{x}_{c,t}; \boldsymbol{x}_{w,t}; \boldsymbol{x}_{F,t}] \quad (1)$$

The sequence $\boldsymbol{x}_c = \{\boldsymbol{x}_{c,t}\}_{t=1}^{M}$ is a sequence of character embeddings corresponding to $\boldsymbol{C}$. Each element of $x_c$, $x_{c,t}$ corresponds to a GloVe embedding (Pennington et al., 2014) for the corresponding character in $\boldsymbol{C}$.

In addition to $\boldsymbol{x}_c$, we also use $\boldsymbol{x}_w$ and $\boldsymbol{x}_F$, which are sequences of word embeddings to integrate the word meanings into the input. $\boldsymbol{x}_w$ is the character-based word sequence, which is a word sequence whose length is the same as that of the character sequence $\boldsymbol{C}$. Let $\boldsymbol{W} = \{w_t\}_{t=1}^{M}$ be a character-based word sequence, where $M$ denotes the number of characters of a word sequence. Here, let $\boldsymbol{S} = \{s_i\}_{i=1}^{N}, (M \geq N)$ be a word sequence in the input document. $\boldsymbol{W}$ is a variation of $\boldsymbol{S}$, which is created by repeating each word $|s_i|$ times where $|s_i|$ denotes the number of characters in the word $s_i$. Note that $w_t$ and $w_{t+1}$ in $\boldsymbol{W}$ are the same value if they come from the same word $s_i$. The sequence $\boldsymbol{x}_w = \{\boldsymbol{x}_{w,t}\}_{t=1}^{M}$ is a sequence of word embeddings corresponding to $\boldsymbol{W}$. Each element of $\{\boldsymbol{x}_{w,t}\}$ is also trained by GloVe (Pennington et al., 2014). The sequence $\boldsymbol{x}_F$ is the alternative version of $\boldsymbol{x}_w$, using the Flair training scheme (Akbik et al., 2018) instead of GloVe.

The input $\boldsymbol{x}$ is given to the LSTM network layer. In this layer, each unit of the LSTM updates the state of the $t$-th element $\boldsymbol{x}_t$ on the basis of the previous LSTM ($\boldsymbol{c}_{t-1}$) and the hidden state ($\boldsymbol{h}_{t-1}$), and outputs the updated state as $\boldsymbol{h}_t$ and $\boldsymbol{c}_t$.

$$\boldsymbol{h}_t, \boldsymbol{c}_t = LSTM(\boldsymbol{x}_t, \boldsymbol{h}_{t-1}, \boldsymbol{c}_{t-1}; \boldsymbol{\theta}) \quad (2)$$

In a BiLSTM network, the output $\overrightarrow{\boldsymbol{h}}$ of the forward LSTM and the output $\overleftarrow{\boldsymbol{h}}$ of the backward LSTM are combined to compute the total output $\overleftrightarrow{\boldsymbol{h}}$.

$$\overleftrightarrow{\boldsymbol{h}} = [\overleftarrow{\boldsymbol{h}}; \overrightarrow{\boldsymbol{h}}] \quad (3)$$

Next, the output of the LSTM network layer, $\overleftrightarrow{\boldsymbol{h}}$, is sent to the next CRF layer. In this layer, the labeling scheme that takes into account the transition probability between labels is carried out, and the output sequence $\boldsymbol{y}$ is calculated against $\boldsymbol{x}$. The output is selected for the optimal sequence on the basis of the Equation (4) where $\phi$ is the feature function and $\boldsymbol{W}_{CRF}$ is a weight coefficient learned in this layer.

$$\boldsymbol{y}^* = \arg\max_{\boldsymbol{y}} \sum_t \boldsymbol{W}_{CRF} \cdot \phi(\overleftrightarrow{\boldsymbol{h}}, y_t, y_{t-1}) \quad (4)$$

The element $y_t$ of the output label sequence $\boldsymbol{y}$ represents the entity label for each character $c_t$. In general, named entity may be composed of multiple characters. So, we use the BIO scheme to represent the chunks of the named entity.

## 4 Proposed Method

The proposed method is a variation of the visual-enhanced BiLSTM-CRF models that enable to integrate visual features into the basic BiLSTM-CRF model described in the previous section. The proposed method utilizes element-wise visual features by obtaining image data for each word in the input document through an image retrieval engine where each word in the document is used as a search query. By retrieving images associated to words, the proposed method can be applied to any documents, while the previous visual-enhanced models mentioned in Section 2 can only be applied to documents with images attached to them.

Figure 3 shows an overview of the proposed method. The left-hand side shows the basic BiLSTM-CRF model. The right-hand side shows the proposed module to create element-wise visual features. In this section, we describe the proposed method step by step. First, we explain the procedure for constructing queries from the input document (Section 4.1). Next, we explain how to obtain visual embeddings (Section 4.2) and integrate the visual features to the original text features (Section 4.3). We then update the input vector sequence shown in Equation (1) to carry the visual features to the BiLSTM-CRF (Section 4.4).

### 4.1 Retrieving Image data

The given input document is transformed into a character-based word sequence $\boldsymbol{W} = \{w_t\}_{t=1}^{M}$ by using the same procedure described in the previous section. Then, we construct a query sequence

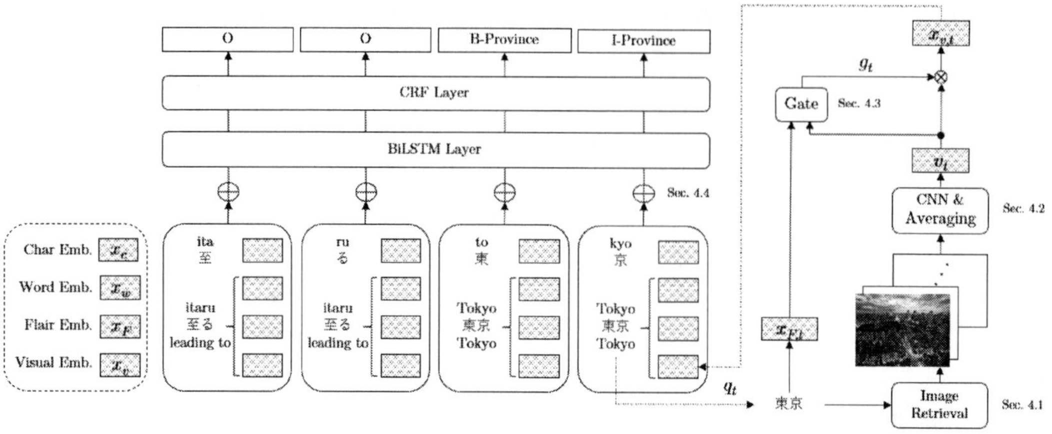


Figure 3: The overview of the proposed model. The left-hand side is the basic BiLSTM-CRF model. The right-hand side is the proposed module to create element-wise visual features.

$\boldsymbol{Q} = \{q_t\}_{t=1}^{M}$: if $w_t$ is a noun, $q_t$ is $w_t$ itself, otherwise $q_t$ is empty. As other word types would be irrelevant for image retrieval, we focus only on nouns. Nouns include not only proper nouns but also common nouns. The part-of-speech information is provided by the Japanese POS tagger MeCab, which is described below.

Each $q_t$ in $\boldsymbol{Q}$ is used as the query for the image retrieval independently of each other; namely, we run the image retrieval $M$ times. The top $K$ retrieved images, referred to as $\boldsymbol{p}_t$, are saved for each run. If a query $q_t$ is empty, no retrievals are performed and $\boldsymbol{p}_t$ is also set to empty. The $\boldsymbol{P} = \{\boldsymbol{p}_t\}_{t=1}^{M}$ is sent to the next step as element-wise visual information.

## 4.2 Obtaining Visual Embeddings

DenseNets (Huang et al., 2016) are one of the most powerful CNN-based deep neural network architectures, especially for image recognition. A pre-trained DenseNet model is applied to the retrieved images $\boldsymbol{p}_t$ to obtain visual embeddings. First, each image in $\boldsymbol{p}_t$ is sent to the DenseNet, and then the hidden representation of the final hidden layer of the DenseNet is saved. After $K$ times running, the average of the $K$ hidden representations is obtained as the visual embedding $\boldsymbol{v}_t$.

If $\boldsymbol{p}_t$ is empty, we define $\boldsymbol{v}_t$ as a *zero* vector where every element is 0.

## 4.3 Combining Visual Embeddings

The obtained visual embedding $\boldsymbol{v}_t$ are modified to adjust the balance of combinations between the original text features and our visual features. Here, we introduce the **Gate mechanism** to control how much of the visual features are input to the BiLSTM-CRF model. It works to decrease the degree of effect of the visual features when retrieved images from polysemous words, abbreviations, and misspellings are inappropriate. We also present another **simple procedure**, which we compared against the Gate mechanism..

**Gate mechanism** This procedure is formulated as follows.

$$\begin{aligned} g_t &= \sigma(\boldsymbol{W}_g \cdot [\boldsymbol{v}_t; \boldsymbol{x}_{F,t}] + b) \\ \boldsymbol{x}_{v,t} &= g_t \boldsymbol{v}_t \end{aligned} \tag{5}$$

The modified visual embedding $\boldsymbol{x}_{v,t}$ is obtained by $\boldsymbol{v}_t$ multiplied by $g_t$. The modification weight $g_t$ is calculated on the basis of the visual feature $\boldsymbol{v}_t$ and the text feature $\boldsymbol{x}_{F,t}$. We use $\boldsymbol{x}_{F,t}$ because the feature relevance $\boldsymbol{v}_t$ and context information around $w_t$ needs to be verified. Here, $\sigma()$ denotes the sigmoid function and $\boldsymbol{W}_g$ and $b$ the weight coefficients to be trained. If a visual feature provides useful context, the $g_t$ is close to 1, otherwise close to 0. Note that no visual features are considered when $g_t = 0$.

**Simple** This procedure is used as a comparison with the Gate mechanism where $\boldsymbol{x}_{v,t}$ is defined as follow.

$$\boldsymbol{x}_{v,t} = \boldsymbol{v}_t \tag{6}$$

Note that this procedure is equivalent to the gate function in which $g_t$ is fixed at 1.

| #words | 5,149,521 |
|---|---|
| #lexicons | 75,024 |
| #documents | 10,158 |
| #sentences | 141,146 |

Table 1: Statistics of ENE corpus

| class | #types | #mentions |
|---|---|---|
| City | 2,936 | 12,687 |
| Country | 431 | 21,340 |
| County | 150 | 248 |
| GPE_Other | 95 | 1,203 |
| Province | 381 | 8,861 |
| MIX | 21 | 66 |

Table 2: Statistics of location name classes

### 4.4 Use of Visual Features

Finally, the input vector sequence shown in Equation (1) is updated to Equation (7) to input the visual features to the input layer of the BiLSTM-CRF.

$$\boldsymbol{x}_t = [\boldsymbol{x}_{c,t}; \boldsymbol{x}_{w,t}; \boldsymbol{x}_{F,t}; \boldsymbol{x}_{v,t}] \tag{7}$$

## 5 Experiments

### 5.1 Dataset

We used the Extended Named Entity corpus (ENE corpus) (Hashimoto et al., 2008), which uses the definition of Sekine's Extended Named Entity Hierarchy (Sekine et al., 2002) 7.1.0 including more than 200 types of named entities including a number of location name types. This corpus is one of the commonly-used datasets for evaluating Japanese NER methods. Each document in the corpus has no attached images. The statistics of ENE corpus are shown in Table 1.

We focused on six classes: Country, Province, County, City, GPE_Other, and MIX in the experiments. The first five classes are the original ones enclosed in Sekine's definition. We included MIX to indicate cases that have multiple NE classes. Hereafter, we ignore MIX for convenience because of rare cases. The statistics of each class are shown in Table 2[1].

Before training, we divided the dataset into three parts: training, develop and test in the ratio

[1] In this study, we found a number of annotation errors in the ENE corpus. We carefully observed 328 mentions related to the location name and corrected them before conducting our experiments.

| class | #M(train) | #M(dev) | #M(test) |
|---|---|---|---|
| City | 8,567 | 2,184 | 1,936 |
| Country | 14,534 | 3,593 | 3,213 |
| County | 172 | 43 | 33 |
| GPE_Other | 848 | 231 | 124 |
| Province | 5,888 | 1,525 | 1,448 |
| MIX | 54 | 9 | 3 |

#M(·) means number of mentions.

Table 3: Statistics of dataset

of 70:15:15. The statistics of dataset are shown in Table 3

### 5.2 Settings

We constructed three models for location name recognition. The first is the baseline model and the others are the proposed models described in Section 4.

- **Baseline** is the BiLSTM-CRF model described in Section 3. No use of visual features.

- **Visual (Gate)** is the proposed visual-enhanced BiLSTM-CRF model that utilizes element-wise visual features with the Gate mechanism.

- **Visual (Simple)** is another proposed model. This model uses the Simple text/visual combination instead of the Gate mechanism.

For word embeddings $\boldsymbol{x}_w$ and character embeddings $\boldsymbol{x}_c$, we conducted the GloVe training with 300 dimensions with the BCCWJ corpus (Maekawa et al., 2014). We use MeCab (Kudo et al., 2004) with the unidic (Den et al., 2007) dictionary for word segmentation. The Flair embeddings (Akbik et al., 2018) were trained using BCCWJ and ten years of Mainichi newspaper data from 1991 to 2000 with 1024 dimensions.

We used Google Images[2] with photo options for the image retrieval used in the proposed models. The top 15 retrieved images for each query are saved. In the dataset, about 43% of words were nouns, enabling non-empty queries to be constructed. The visual embeddings were created from the final hidden layer representation of DenseNet, whose dimensions were 1024. We used the pre-trained DenseNet from PyTorch.

[2] https://images.google.com/

| Model | Prec. | Recall | F1 |
|---|---|---|---|
| Baseline | 87.33 | 89.47 | 88.38 |
| Visual (Simple) | **90.20** | 87.78 | 88.97* |
| Visual (Gate) | 89.33 | **90.01** | **89.67**** |

We performed an approximate randomization test (Chinchor, 1992) on the F1 values. The mark "*" and "**" in the table show significant differences compared with the baseline at the 0.05 and 0.01 levels, respectively.

Table 4: Experimental Results

In the training of the models, we used Adam (Kingma and Ba, 2014) for optimization. The batch size was 20. We applied the dropout regularization (Srivastava et al., 2014) at $p = 0.5$ for each node of the input layer and each output node of the LSTM layer. We also used a gradient clipping (Pascanu et al., 2013) of 1.0 to reduce the effects of the gradient exploding.

We used the standard BIO schema (Tjong Kim Sang and Veenstra, 1999) for the chunk representation. The performance was measured by the Precision (Prec.), Recall, and F1 values. Only the exact matches were counted as the correct samples, while lenient matches were counted as incorrect.

### 5.3 Results and Discussion

Experimental results are shown in Table 4. Both models using element-wise visual features outperformed the baseline model. This result suggests that element-wise visual features are powerful features for location name recognition. Furthermore, the Visual (Gate) model achieved the best F1 value of 89.67%. From the results, the Gate mechanism is an essential part of integrating element-wise visual features into the baseline model.

The following example sentences are samples in the cases where the Visual (Gate) has a correct output while the Baseline has an incorrect output. Here, (1-J) and (2-J) are the original Japanese sentences, and (1-E) and (2-E) are the corresponding English translations.

- (ex.1-J) １９８２年１２月の**ジャマイカ** $_{Country}$ における最終議定書及び条約署名会議において１１７か国及び２地域が署名し成立した

- (ex.1-E) Signed by 117 countries and two regions at the Final Protocol and Convention Signing Conference in **Jamaica**$_{Country}$ in December 1982.

- (ex.2-J) いよいよ、明日は、帰る日を除いて、フランス滞在の最終日です。**アヴィニヨン** $_{City}$ に行く予定です。

- (ex.2-E) Finally, tomorrow is the last day of our stay in France, except for the day we leave. We're going to **Avignon**$_{City}$.

Figure 4: An example photo retrieved by the query ジャマイカ (Jamaica).

Figure 5: An example photo retrieved by the query アヴィニヨン (Avignon).

In the first example, ジャマイカ (Jamaica) is a country name to be recognized, and in the second example, アヴィニヨン (Avignon) is a city name in France. Moreover, the examples of retrieved image data corresponding to these location names are shown in Figure 4 and Figure 5, respectively. One can see that a typical scene or object is in each image; a beach in Figure 4 and a palace in Figure 5. It suggests that image data showing scenes or objects strongly relevant to locations provide helpful visual features.

Table 5 shows the fine-grained performances of the experimental results. It shows that the City class had the most significant improvement. In fact, we confirmed that the retrieved image data corresponding to city names showed many typical characteristics of the locations, such as buildings, landscapes, and skies. In contrast, for an example of other classes, image data corresponding to country names showed various weakly related objects to the countries. For example, we found some image data showing the president of its country.

| class | Prec. | Recall | F1 |
|---|---|---|---|
| | Baseline | | |
| City | 84.18 | 77.90 | 80.92 |
| Country | 89.88 | 96.29 | 92.97 |
| County | 83.78 | 93.94 | 88.57 |
| GPE_Other | 85.90 | 75.28 | 80.24 |
| Province | 85.40 | 90.24 | 87.75 |
| | Visual(Simple) | | |
| City | 87.67 | 78.16 | 82.64 |
| Country | 93.07 | 93.68 | 93.37 |
| County | 82.35 | 84.85 | 83.58 |
| GPE_Other | 82.72 | 75.28 | 78.82 |
| Province | 87.37 | 88.10 | 87.73 |
| | Visual(Gate) | | |
| City | 89.38 | 78.67 | 83.68 |
| Country | 91.74 | 95.81 | 93.73 |
| County | 93.55 | 87.88 | 90.62 |
| GPE_Other | 84.42 | 73.03 | 78.31 |
| Province | 84.55 | 93.15 | 88.64 |

Table 5: Performance for each class

These seem to suggest not location names but person names.

Here we call words that appear in test data but not in training data as unseen words. In general, it is arduous to achieve accurate NER performance on unseen words because they do not appear in training data and thus have poor textual information. Here, we investigated whether our visual features provide supplemental information to unseen words. To realize the investigation, we conducted an analysis focusing on the City class. As shown in Table 2, the City class differs from other classes in that it has many types of mentions. It implies that there are many unseen mentions to be recognized to the City class. Therefore we compared the extraction performance between seen words and unseen words in the City class. Table 6 shows the details of the results. One can see that the unseen words achieved better performance improvements than the seen words. Furthermore, precision values improved most significantly (Seen(+5.08) $\rightarrow$ Unseen(+7.07)). This means that visual features improve the performance of not only true-positive samples but also true-negative samples. The example sentences are shown below. Each underline indicates the unseen true-negative word. And, the corresponding retrieved images are shown in Figure 6 and Figure 7. These samples were correctly classified by the proposed method while wrongly

Figure 6: An example photo retrieved by the query ブンデスリーガ (Bundesliga).

Figure 7: An example photo retrieved by the query シスコ (Cisco).

by the baseline method.

- (ex.3-J) ドイツ・ブンデスリーガの強豪、バイエルン・ミュンヘンと「アドバイザー契約」を結んで４年目。
- (ex.3-E) This is the fourth year that he has signed an "advisory contract" with German Bundesliga powerhouse Bayern Munich
- (ex.4-J) このような……シスコの経営陣は……
- (ex.4-E) This kind of... Cisco's management team...

Although, as discussed above, the element-wise visual features contributed to improve the performance of location name recognition, some types of errors remained. It observed that the proposed method tends to cause false-positive errors in compound words including location names. For example, 京都-議定書 (the Kyoto Protocol) in (5-J) and (5-E) was wrongly recognized as the location name. This type of error is caused by inadequate query construction. Because every single noun in the document is regarded as the query word independently in the proposed method, both 京都 (Kyoto) and 議定書 (Protocol) were used to the image retrievals. Then they led to the mistaken recognition of Kyoto.

- (ex.5-J) 温室効果ガス削減に向け、政府が決めた京都議定書の目標達成計画には様々な方策が並んでいる。

| | Model | Precision | Recall | F1 |
|---|---|---|---|---|
| Seen | Baseline | 84.99 | 79.29 | 82.04 |
| | Visual (Gate) | 90.07 (+5.08) | 80.05 (+0.76) | 84.77 (+2.73) |
| Unseen | Baseline | 68.54 | 54.95 | 61.0 |
| | Visual (Gate) | 75.61 (+7.07) | 55.86 (+0.91) | 64.25 (+3.25) |

Table 6: Comparison between seen & unseen mentions for City class

Figure 8: An example photo retrieved by the query アンゴラ (Angola). This photo shows not " Angola " but " Angora rabbit " .

- (ex.5-E) The government's plan to meet the Kyoto Protocol's targets for reducing greenhouse gas emissions includes a number of measures.

It also observed that the proposed method tends to cause false-negative errors when inappropriate images are mixed to the retrieved images. For example, the proposed method missed recognizing アンゴラ (Angola) in (6-J) and (6-E) because the image data retrieved by the query アンゴラ (Angola) includes some inappropriate images of "Angora rabbit" like in Figure 8. アンゴラ (Angola) is not a polysemous word, but it found that the word means "Angora rabbit" in the specific domain [3].

- (ex.6-J) 内戦の続く**アンゴラ**$_{Country}$ではコレラが流行。

- (ex.6-E) Cholera epidemic in **Angola**$_{Country}$ as civil war continues.

## 6 Conclusion

In this study, we proposed a NER model that uses images corresponding to all nouns in a document as features and a Gate mechanism that controls the extent to which visual features are provided as input to the neural NER model. We conducted experiments to confirm its performance in location name recognition. Experimental results show that the proposed method achieved a higher F1-value performance than the baseline model in the ENE corpus dataset, with a significant difference of $p < 0.01$.

In future research, we will investigate whether the proposed model is effective for cases other than location names. We also aim to improve our model to be more effective by conducting elaborate query investigations that are motivated by the error analysis. The hyper-parameter $K$, which means the number of images per word, would be critical for obtaining valuable visual embeddings. Therefore, we will also investigate whether the larger the $K$, the better the location name recognition performance. The experimental results showed that the proposed method has little contributions when query words are polysemous. We would like to attempt word sequence queries with nouns and adjectives/verbs instead of single noun queries.

## Acknowledgments

We thank anonymous reviewers for their responsible attitude and helpful comments. This work was supported by JSPS KAKENHI Grant Number JP18K11982.

## References

Alan Akbik, Duncan Blythe, and Roland Vollgraf. 2018. Contextual String Embeddings for Sequence Labeling. In *Proceedings of the 27th International Conference on Computational Linguistics*, pages 1638–1649.

Meysam Asgari-Chenaghlu, M. Reza Feizi-Derakhshi, Leili Farzinvash, M. A. Balafar, and Cina Motamed. 2020. A multimodal deep learning approach for named entity recognition from social media. https://arxiv.org/abs/2001.06888.

Nancy Chinchor. 1992. The Statistical Significance of the MUC-4 Results. In *Proceedings of*

[3]Note that the words "Angola" and "Angora" are transliterated into the same Japanese string "アンゴラ" although they are different in English.

*the Fourth Message Uunderstanding Conference (MUC-4)*, page 30–50.

Jim Cowie and Wendy Lehnert. 1996. Information extraction. *Communications of the ACM*, 39(1):80–91.

Yasuharu Den, Toshinobu Ogiso, Hideki Ogura, Atsushi Yamada, Nobuaki Minematsu, Kiyotaka Uchimoto, and Hanae Koiso. 2007. electronic dictionary, morphological analysis, database system, uniformity of units, identity of indexes. *Japanese Linguistics*, pages 101–123.

Ralph Grishman and Beth Sundheim. 1996. Message Understanding Conference-6. In *Proceedings of the 16th conference on Computational linguistics*, page 466–471.

Taiichi Hashimoto, Takashi Inui, and Koji Murakami. 2008. Constructing extended named entity annotated corpora. *IPSJ SIG Notes*, pages 113–120.

Gao Huang, Zhuang Liu, Laurens van der Maaten, and Kilian Q. Weinberger. 2016. Densely Connected Convolutional Networks. https://arxiv.org/abs/1608.06993.

Zhiheng Huang, Wei Xu, and Kai Yu. 2015. Bidirectional LSTM-CRF Models for Sequence Tagging. https://arxiv.org/abs/1508.01991.

Yaozong Jia and Xiaopan Ma. 2019. Attention in Character-Based BiLSTM-CRF for Chinese Named Entity Recognition. In *ICMAI 2019 Proceedings of the 2019 4th International Conference on Mathematics and Artificial Intelligence*, page 1–4.

Diederik P. Kingma and Jimmy Ba. 2014. Adam: A method for stochastic optimization. https://arxiv.org/abs/1412.6980.

Taku Kudo, Kaoru Yamamoto, and Yuji Matsumoto. 2004. Applying Conditional Random Fields to Japanese Morphologiaical Analysis. *IPSJ SIG Notes*, 161:89–96.

Guillaume Lample, Miguel Ballesteros, Sandeep Subramanian, Kazuya Kawakami, and Chris Dyer. 2016. Neural Architectures for Named Entity Recognition. In *Proceedings of the 2016 Conference of the North American Chapter of the Association for Computational Linguistics: Human Language Technologies*, pages 260–270.

Jing Li, Aixin Sun, Jianglei Han, and Chenliang Li. 2018. A Survey on Deep Learning for Named Entity Recognition. https://arxiv.org/abs/1812.09449.

Di Lu, Leonardo Neves, Vitor Carvalho, Ning Zhang, and Heng Ji. 2018. Visual Attention Model for Name Tagging in Multimodal Social Media. In *Proceedings of the 56th Annual Meeting of the Association for Computational Linguistics*, pages 1990–1999.

Kikuo Maekawa, Makoto Yamazaki, Toshinobu Ogiso, Takehiko Maruyama, Hideki Ogura, Wakako Kashino, Hanae Koiso, Masaya Yamaguchi, Makiro Tanaka, and Yasuharu Den. 2014. Balanced corpus of contemporary written Japanese. *Language Resources and Evaluation*, 48:345–371.

Michał Marcińczuk. 2015. Automatic construction of complex features in Conditional Random Fields for Named Entities Recognition. In *Proceedings of the International Conference Recent Advances in Natural Language Processing*, pages 413–419.

Shotaro Misawa, Motoki Taniguchi, and Yasuhide Miura. 2017. Character-based Bidirectional LSTM-CRF with words and characters for Japanese Named Entity Recognition. In *Proceedings of the First Workshop on Subword and Character Level Models in NLP*, pages 97–102.

Seungwhan Moon, Leonardo Neves, and Vitor Carvalho. 2019. Multimodal Named Entity Recognition for Short Social Media Posts. In *Proceedings of the 2018 Conference of the North American Chapter of the Association for Computational Linguistics: Human Language Technologies*, pages 852–860.

Razvan Pascanu, Tomas Mikolov, and Yoshua Bengio. 2013. On the difficulty of training recurrent neural networks. In *Proceedings of the 30th International Conference on International Conference on Machine Learning*, page III–1310–III–1318.

Jeffrey Pennington, Richard Socher, and Christopher Manning. 2014. GloVe: Global Vectors for Word Representation. In *Proceedings of the 2014 Conference on Empirical Methods in Natural Language Processing*, pages 1532–1543.

Satoshi Sekine, Kiyoshi Sudo, and Chikashi Nobata. 2002. Extended named entity hierarchy. In *Proceedings of the Third International Conference on Language Resources and Evaluation*.

Nitish Srivastava, Geoffrey Hinton, Alex Krizhevsky, Ilya Sutskever, and Ruslan Salakhutdinov. 2014. Dropout: A simple way to prevent neural networks from overfitting. *Journal of Machine Learning Research*, page 1929–1958.

Erik F. Tjong Kim Sang and Jorn Veenstra. 1999. Representing Text Chunks. In *Proceedings of the Ninth Conference of the European Chapter of the Association for Computational Linguistics*, page 173–179.

Davy Weissenbacher, Arjun Magge, Karen O'Connor, Matthew Scotch, and Graciela Gonzalez-Hernandez. 2019. SemEval-2019 Task 12: Toponym Resolution in Scientific Papers. In *Proceedings of the 13th International Workshop on Semantic Evaluation*, pages 907–916.

Qi Zhang, Jinlan Fu, Xiaoyu Liu, and Xuanjing Huang. 2018. Adaptive co-attention network for named entity recognition in tweets. In *Proceedings of the Thirty-Second AAAI Conference on Artificial Intelligence, (AAAI-18)*, pages 5674–5681.

# BERT-based Spatial Information Extraction

Hyeong Jin Shin[*], Jeong Yeon Park[**], Dae Bum Yuk[**], Jae Sung Lee[**]

Computer Science Major, School of Electrical Engineering and Computer Science,
Graduate School of Chungbuk National University, Korea

hjshin1985@gmail.com[*], {parkjeongyeon, daebum1994, jasonlee}@cbnu.ac.kr[**]

## Abstract

Spatial information extraction is essential to understand geographical information in text. This task is largely divided to two subtasks: spatial element extraction and spatial relation extraction. In this paper, we utilize BERT (Devlin et al., 2018), which is very effective for many natural language processing applications. We propose a BERT-based spatial information extraction model, which uses BERT for spatial element extraction and R-BERT (Wu and He, 2019) for spatial relation extraction. The model was evaluated with the SemEval 2015 dataset. The result showed a 15.4% point increase in spatial element extraction and an 8.2% point increase in spatial relation extraction in comparison to the baseline model (Nichols and Botros, 2015).

## 1 Introduction

Extracting spatial relations from text is a type of relation extraction, focusing on the static and dynamic spatial relations in the text. It is essential for natural language understanding systems, such as robot navigation systems and question-answering systems, to understand geographical relations or to track moving objects.

For example, in the sentence, "Tom is on the box," we find a static relation in which *Tom* is the trajector, *box* is the landmark, and *on* denotes their static spatial relation. In the following sentence, "He steps down from the box to the ground," we also find a dynamic spatial relation, in which *He (Tom)* is the mover, *steps down* is the trigger, *box* is the source, and *ground* is the destination. Using simple inference based on the extracted relations, we can infer a new relation: "Tom is on the ground now."

The task is largely divided into two subtasks[1]: spatial element extraction and spatial relation extraction. Finding candidate elements for spatial relations roles, such as the trajector, landmark, and trigger, defines spatial element extraction. Finding or verifying relations among the role candidates defines spatial relation extraction.

Many natural language processing techniques and machine learning methods have been applied to spatial information extraction. For example, a conditional random field (CRF) model (Lafferty et al., 2001) is used for spatial element extraction, and support vector machine (SVM) (Suykens and Vandewalle, 1999; Roberts and Haragagiu, 2012) and convolutional neural net (CNN) (Mazalov et al., 2015) models are used for spatial relation extraction. Various language resources, such as GloVe (Pennington et al., 2014), WordNet (Salaberri et al., 2015), and PropBank (Salaberri et al., 2015) are also used for spatial information extraction.

In this paper, we propose a BERT-based spatial information extraction model that utilizes BERT (Devlin et al., 2018) extensively for both spatial element extraction and spatial relation extraction. Recently, many context-aware language models have been developed, including not only BERT, but also ELMO (Peters et al., 2018), XLNet (Yang et al., 2019), and GPT (Radford et al., 2018), among others. We chose BERT simply because many downstream applications of the BERT system have been developed for named entity

[1] The subtasks are defined in more detail for evaluation in SemEval-2015 Task 8 (Pustejovsky et al., 2015). Spatial element extraction and spatial relation extraction correspond to 1.b and 1.d tasks, respectively, in the definition. However, in this paper, spatial element extraction task is extended to extract not only spatial elements such as paths, places, motions, spatial entities, for instance, but also spatial signals and motion signals.



*Proceedings of the Third International Workshop on Spatial Language Understanding (SpLU 2020)*, pages 10–17
November 19, 2020. ©2020 Association for Computational Linguistics
https://doi.org/10.18653/v1/P17

recognition and semantic role labeling, which can be easily applied to spatial information extraction.

In Section 2, we briefly summarize related works. In Section 3, we describe our proposed model, which consists of three modules, specifically a spatial element extraction model, a triple candidate generator, and a spatial relation extraction model. Section 4 presents the experimental results of our model. Finally, section 5 concludes the paper.

## 2 Related Works

An early method of spatial information extraction was introduced as spatial role labeling (SpRL) by Kordjamshidi et al. (2011). SemEval-2012 introduced a spatial role labeling task mainly focusing on static spatial relations. SemEval-2013 expanded static spatial relations to capture fine-grained semantics and to include dynamic spatial relations.

SemEval-2015 was the first shared task conference to evaluate implementation systems for the SpaceEval annotation scheme, which is the current spatial information annotation scheme (Pustejovsky et al., 2015). Many spatial information extraction systems have been developed based on the SpaceEval annotation scheme.

Nichols and Botros (2015) proposed the SpRL-CWW model, which uses a CRF model (Lafferty et al., 2001) for spatial element extraction and an SVM model (Suykens and Vandewalle, 1999) for spatial relation extraction. It uses many input features for element extraction, such as word embedding using GloVe (Pennington et al., 2014), named entities, part of speech tags and dependency parse labels. SVM is used to filter out correct triples from all possible combinations of triples. D'Souza and Ng (2015) proposed the UTD-SpRL model based on SVM, which includes more than 100 different features generated by a greedy feature selection technique and uses the joint detection of a relation's arguments. The X-Space model proposed by Salaberri et al. (2015) uses node information, such as the place, position, location and so forth, included in WordNet for spatial element extraction. It also uses argument information in PropBank for spatial relation classification.

A multimodal approach that uses image and text information simultaneously in a multimodal spatial role labeling (mSpRL) shared task was also presented in CLEF 2017 (Kordjamshidi et al., 2017), but the result was not satisfactory (Zablocki et al., 2017).

Mazalov et al. (2015) extracted spatial roles and their relations by adapting a convolutional neural network based system developed for semantic role labeling. The pre-existing system was successfully adapted to spatial information extraction.

Dan et al. (2020) proposed spatial BERT to predict the spatial relation between two entities given an image involving them. The spatial BERT was composed of a spatial model, implemented with a feed forward network, and a language model, which were implemented with BERT. The language model is used as complementary features to predict unseen (untrained) relations in images. Despite the fact that BERT is used as the language model in this approach, spatial relation extraction is limited to relation detection for the given subject and object entities in the image. Our approach also uses BERT but deals instead with the entire process of relation extraction from raw text; we extract spatial elements from raw text, determine their corresponding spatial roles, and find spatial relations from the spatial roles.

## 3 Spatial Information Extraction Model

We divide the spatial information extraction task into two subtasks: spatial element extraction and spatial relation extraction, according to the ISOspace annotation scheme (ISO, 2014; Pustejovsky et al., 2015). For the integrated system, we pipelined the two subtasks via a triple candidate generator.

Figure 1 shows the overall architecture of our system. A sentence is inputted to the element extractor, which is jointed with one of link's role modules. The element extractor outputs the spatial elements and spatial roles jointly. The spatial roles are combined to triples as spatial relation candidates by the triple candidate generator. The triple candidates are classified as either valid relations or invalid relations by the relation extractor. Each module is described in the following sections.

For the general architecture of spatial relation extraction, two restrictions are imposed in this work. First, only three arguments are allowed. According to ISOspace, we have certain arguments for each relation, as shown Table 1. To maintain the static architecture of relation extraction, we set the number of arguments of each relation to three.

Therefore, we keep all arguments for QSLink (Qualitative Spatial Link), OLink (Orientation information Link), and MeLink (Measurement Link), but for MvLnk (Movement Link), we choose three arguments out of seven: *mover*, *goal*, and *motion*.

Second, only one prime spatial role is determined in the element extraction stage. In multiple relations in a sentence, an entity may be related to multiple relations in multiple roles. In this case, it is necessary to choose only one role in a typical case. For example, in the sentence in Figure 2, 'vase' has two roles for each relation: *trajector* and *landmark*. Because sharing these two different roles most frequently occurs, we decided to include these roles as one role label, *traLand*. The triple candidate generator interprets this role label as two roles separately, *trajector* and *landmark*, for triple candidate generation.

| | | |
|---|---|---|
| Spatial relation | QSLink | **trajector, landmark, trigger** |
| | OLink | **trajector, landmark, trigger** |
| | MvLink | **mover, goal, motion,** midpoint, landmark, source, path |
| | MeLink | **trajector, landmark, measure** |

Table 1: Spatial roles of each link

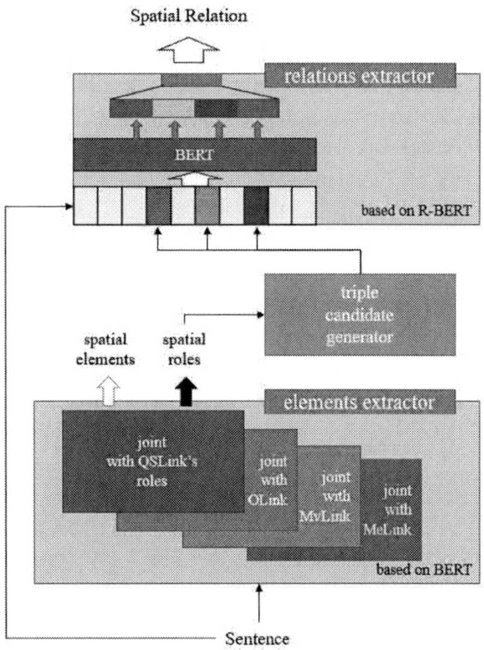


Figure 1: Pipeline model for spatial information extraction

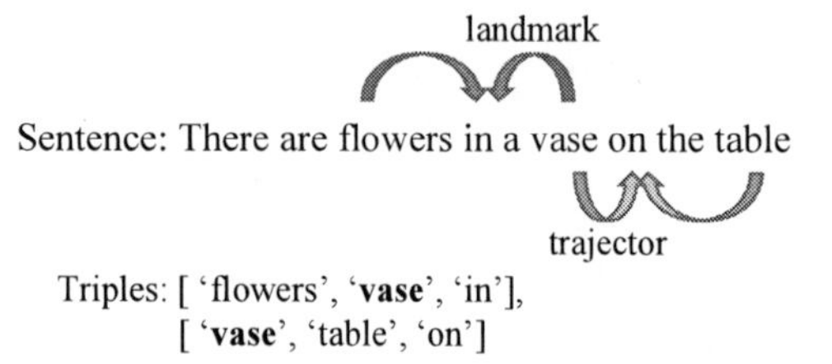


Figure 2: Example of sharing *trajector* and *landmark* roles: *vase* has two roles, *trajector* and *landmark*

### 3.1 Spatial Element Extraction

Spatial element extraction is a problem of sequence labeling, which can be easily solved with BERT. The structure of the model is shown in Figure 3. A sentence is segmented into word pieces and they are inputted to BERT to extract the spatial elements and spatial roles jointly. In previous methods, many features are extracted through preprocessing for learning by CRFs (Nichols and Botros, 2015). However, the BERT-based spatial element extraction module does not require any preprocessing for feature extraction; rather, it requires only raw text as input for fine tuning.

Multi-layer perceptron (MLP), used for a classifier on top of BERT, performs fully connected layer computation and produces IOB-based tags for annotation. Because BERT is based on word pieces (Wu et al., 2016), the outputs are also word pieces. For sequence labeling, we labeled only the first word piece. For example, we can assume that 'flower' is divided into two word pieces 'flow' and '##er', with only 'flow' then annotated as a normal tag, such as a Spatial Entity tag, whereas '##er' is annotated as an Other tag.

We use a joint model for spatial element extraction and spatial role extraction. Two classifiers are located on top of the BERT system and share the same parameters for BERT fine tuning. We noted an improvement in the joint model over the single model during a preliminary test on Korean data (Kim and Lee, 2016).

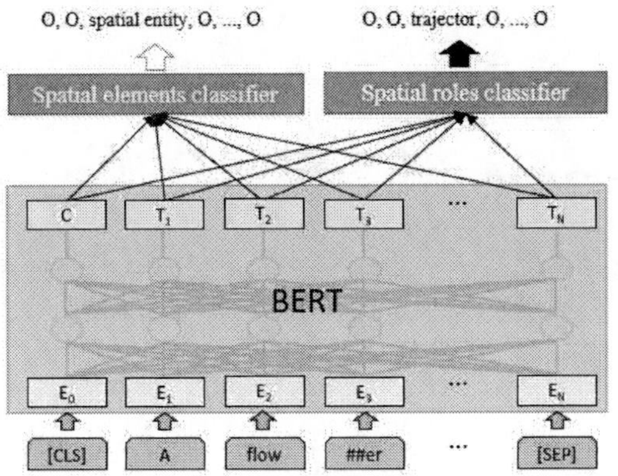

Figure 3: Joint model for spatial elements and spatial role extraction

### 3.2 Triple Candidate Generator

Because the spatial role extractor produces only entity tags, we do not know which entity is related to which entity, especially when there are multiple relations. Moreover, we do not know the relation type to which they belong. The triple candidate generator produces all possible combinations of given spatial roles for the spatial relation extractor to determine which combination and type should be chosen.

For example, in the sentence shown in Figure 4, we have two trajectors, 'bike' and 'puppy'; two landmarks, 'warehouse' and 'gate'; and two triggers, 'by' and 'in front of'. The triple candidate generator produces all combinations of trajector, landmark, and trigger. In this case, it produces 8 (2*2*2) triple candidates. Generally, for a set of trajector T, a set of landmark L, and a set of trigger G, we have a number of Cartesian product triple candidates: |T|*|L|*|G|.

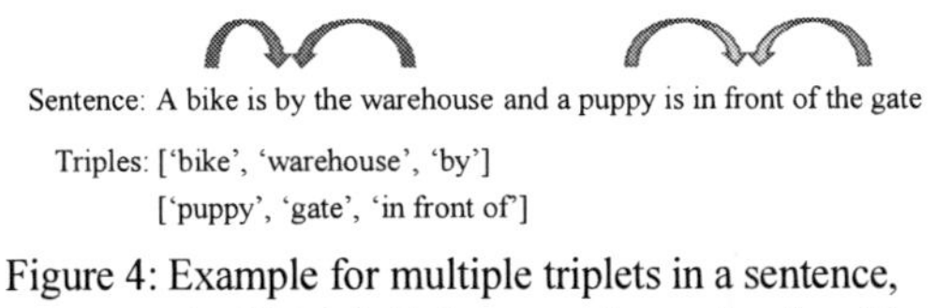

Figure 4: Example for multiple triplets in a sentence, represented with triple [*trigger*, *trajector*, *landmark*]

### 3.3 Spatial Relation Extraction

Spatial relation extraction is a task to identify the relation between given entities, in our case, triple entities. A similar task has been done by using BERT in semantic role labeling (SRL), in which a relationship is classified for two given semantic role arguments (Wu and He, 2019). This model showed the best performance in SRL, and we refer to this model as R-BERT in this paper. We adopted R-BERT for spatial relation extraction, but we modified two aspects of the model. We extended two arguments to three arguments, and we include null argument for the case of a movement link.

Figure 5 shows the structure of the modified model. A sentence, marked with a triple candidate, is inputted to BERT. The BERT outputs of each of the roles in a triple and CLS token are averaged and go through the fully connected network. The four outputs are concatenated and then go through fully connected network again. The *softmax* of the output is the final result to determine the validity of the triple relation.

For the argument span, the input format is changed with the start index and end index along with the words [words, start index, end index]. In the case of two arguments, we utilize formulae (1) to (5) for the spans of $i$ and $j$, and $k$ and $m$:

$$H'_0 = W_0(\tanh(H_0)) + b_0 \tag{1}$$

$$H'_1 = W_1[\tanh\left(\frac{1}{j-i+1}\sum_{t=i}^{j} H_t\right)] + b_1 \tag{2}$$

$$H'_2 = W_2[\tanh\left(\frac{1}{m-k+1}\sum_{t=k}^{m} H_t\right)] + b_2 \tag{3}$$

$$h'' = W_3[concat(H'_0 + H'_1 + H'_2)] + b_3 \tag{4}$$

$$p = softmax(h'') \tag{5}$$

We extended the model to operate for three arguments of spatial information extraction. We added one additional *tanh* output for a trigger with span $q$ and $r$, as shown in formula (6). We also modified formula (4) to formula (7) to include the trigger:

$$H'_3 = W_4[\tanh\left(\frac{1}{r-q+1}\sum_{t=r}^{q} H_t\right)] + b_4 \tag{6}$$

$$h'' = W_3[concat(H'_0 + H'_1 + H'_2 + H'_3)] + b_3 \tag{7}$$

For the null argument in the case of a movement link, we utilize the last character in the sentence. For example, the sentence "John leaves from school." contains a *mover*, "John," and a *motion*, "leaves," but it does not have a *goal*. In this case, we represent the *goal* as the null argument. Therefore, we have a three-argument span: ['John', 0, 0], ['.', 4, 4], and ['leaves', 1, 1].

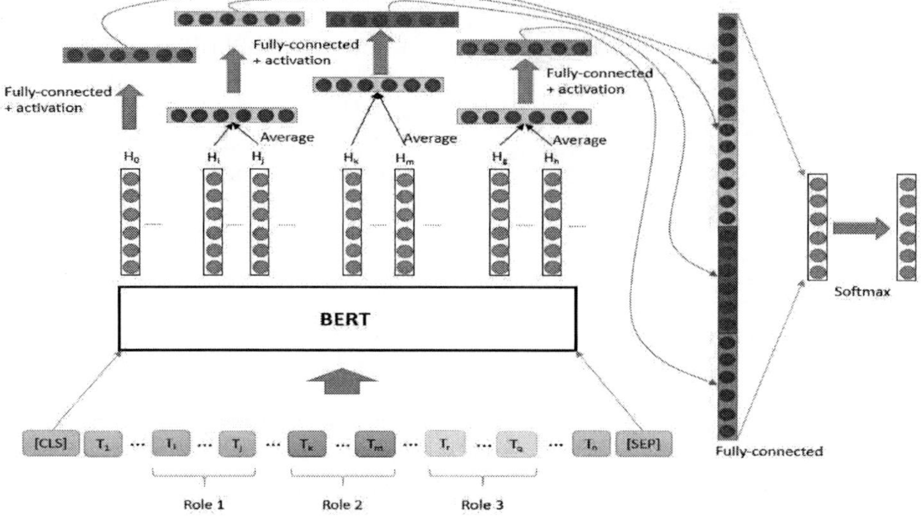


Figure 5: Spatial relation extraction model using R-BERT

## 4 Experiments

### 4.1 Settings and dataset

We use the pre-trained cased $BERT_{BASE}$ version model for fine tuning available at the GitHub site[2]. For both the spatial element model and the relation role extraction model, the hyper-parameters in Table 2 are used.

An experiment was conducted with a dataset of SemEval-2015 task 8: SpaceEval. Table 3 shows the statistics of the dataset.

Because non-motion events and MeLink are usually not evaluated in spatial information extraction tasks, they were excluded from our experiment. We also added invalid triplets generated by the triple candidate generator for training. These triplets accounted for approximately 40% of all data and were used as negative data in the training data.

| Batch size | 1 |
|---|---|
| Learning rate | 2e-5 |
| Hidden size | 768 |
| Dropout rate | 0.1 |

Table 2: Hyper-parameters for BERT element extraction

| place | path | spatial entity | measure |
|---|---|---|---|
| 2,175 | 561 | 1,746 | 201 |
| motion | motion signal | spatial signal | non-motion |
| 940 | 674 | 939 | 418 |

| QSLink | OLink | MvLink | MeLink |
|---|---|---|---|
| 1,005 | 251 | 783 | 74 |

Table 3: Number of spatial elements and relations in the SpaceEval dataset

### 4.2 Results

Because the SpRL-CWW model (Nichols and Botros, 2015) was best in SpaceEval, it was used as the baseline model in this evaluation. In our model, spatial elements and spatial roles are jointly trained and extracted. Because the spatial roles depend on the link relation type, we have four types of joint models here: QSLink, OLink, MvLink, and MeLink. The evaluation results for these models are shown in Table 4. Overall, the performance for element extraction was better than that for role extraction. Moreover, the Joint-with-QSLink model showed the worst performance, whereas the Joint-with-MeLink model showed the best performance.

[2] bert-base-cased model : github.com/google-research/bert

| Joint models | elements | | | roles | | |
|---|---|---|---|---|---|---|
| | prec | rec | F1 | prec | rec | F1 |
| Joint w/ QSLink | 96.1 | 84.5 | 90.0 | 93.1 | 78.6 | 85.2 |
| Joint w/ OLink | 94.8 | 86.8 | 90.6 | 86.7 | 84.0 | 85.3 |
| Joint w/ MvLink | 93.2 | 88.2 | 90.6 | 96.8 | 91.0 | 93.8 |
| Joint w/ MeLink | 95.2 | 88.4 | 91.7 | 97.3 | 97.3 | 97.3 |
| average | 94.8 | 87.0 | 90.7 | 93.5 | 87.7 | 90.4 |

Table 4: Precision, recall and F1 scores of both spatial element and role extraction

Table 5 shows a performance comparison for all elements of the baseline model and our model. The performance was compared with our Joint-with-QSLink model, which showed the worst performance. The results show that the performance of every spatial element increased significantly in comparison with the baseline model. Additionally, the micro-average of our model was 15.4% point better than that of the baseline model. This demonstrates that the BERT-based deep-learning model for element extraction can more effectively improve the performance compared to traditional machine-learning models, such as CRF models, which use features extracted through various preprocessors.

| Spatial Elements | baseline | ours | Δ (ours - base) |
|---|---|---|---|
| Place | 74.7 | 86.8 | +12.1 |
| Path | 61.7 | 94.9 | +33.2 |
| Spatial entity | 80.8 | 89.9 | +9.1 |
| Motion | 76.9 | 94.3 | +17.4 |
| Motion signal | 78.6 | 90.7 | +12.1 |
| Spatial signal | 70.9 | 85.9 | +15.0 |
| Measure | 79.1 | 98.3 | +19.2 |
| Non-motion | 56.4 | 89.4 | +33.0 |
| Micro-average | 74.6 | 90.0 | +15.4 |

Table 5: Performance comparison of spatial element extraction (F1 score)

Table 6 shows a comparison of the spatial relation extraction performance outcomes of selected models. We measured their average performances for only three link types (QSLink, OLink, and MvLink) because a researcher investigating other previous models chose them for evaluation. (Even though the relation type was limited to static relations in SemEval-2012 and SemEval-2013, we included the two best research results, those of Roberts and Haragagiu (2012) and Mazalov et al. (2015), for comparison.) Our model outperformed all of the other models compared here. This proves that our relation classification model based on R-BERT is very effective for spatial relation extraction.

| Models and techniques | prec. | recall | F1 | Δ(F1) |
|---|---|---|---|---|
| Baseline (Nichols and Botros, 2015) CRF/SVM | 56.0 | 51.0 | 53.0 | 0.0 |
| Salaberri et al. (2015) WordNet | 54.0 | 51.0 | 53.0 | 0.0 |
| Roberts and Haragagiu (2012) † SVM | 60.3 | 53.4 | 56.6 | +3.6 |
| Mazalov et al. (2015) ‡ CNN | 60.5 | 56.2 | 58.3 | +5.3 |
| Proposed BERT | 62.7 | 59.8 | 61.2 | +8.2 |

Table 6: Spatial relation extraction performance for comparison

†: SemEval 2012 dataset, relation with general type

‡: SemEval-2013 dataset, average of two datasets

### 4.3 Ablation study

In order to observe the effects of the proposed features, in this case the *traLand* tag, and the joint model of the spatial elements and roles, we conducted an ablation test. Table 7 shows the result. The simple spatial role extraction model (w/o a joint model in the table) performs very poorly at 25.2% F1. Our analysis shows that this occurs because the data for some roles are very sparse in the SemEval dataset, degrading the performance. This problem is mitigated in the joint model with the use of the element data.

The model without *traLand* tag is tested in two ways: replacing the tag with a *trajactor* tag and doing so with a *landmark* tag. The two models are degraded by 22.5% point F1 and by 14.8% point F1, respectively.

These results show that the two proposed features had a positive impact on the performance.

In particular, the joint model feature greatly improved the performance.

| models | prec | recall | F1 | Δ (F1) |
|---|---|---|---|---|
| proposed | 62.7 | 59.8 | 61.2 | 0 |
| w/o joint | 25.7 | 24.6 | 25.2 | -36.0 |
| w/o *traLand* (repl w/ *trajector*) | 26.5 | 71.6 | 38.7 | -22.5 |
| w/o *traLand* (repl w/ *landmark*) | 43.5 | 49.7 | 46.4 | -14.8 |

Table 7. Ablation test of models without using the joint training feature and a dual-role tag (*traLand*)

## 5 Conclusion

Spatial information extraction is necessary for many applications, such as robot navigation and question-answering systems, to understand geographical information in text. This task is processed largely with two subtasks: spatial element extraction and spatial relation extraction.

In this paper, we proposed a BERT-based spatial information extraction model that uses BERT (Devlin et al., 2018) for spatial element extraction and R-BERT (Wu and He, 2019) for spatial relation extraction. The two modules are connected with a pipeline through a triple candidate generator.

Spatial elements are extracted jointly with spatial roles that are input for spatial relation extraction. The joint model contributes to increase the performance of spatial role extraction in some cases, which is more useful for relation extraction. R-BERT, which was originally used for semantic role labeling, was modified here to handle three arguments and a null argument for spatial relation extraction.

Our model was evaluated with the SemEval 2015 dataset. The result showed a 15.4% point improvement in spatial element extraction and an 8.2% point improvement in spatial relation extraction in comparison to the baseline model (Nichols and Botros, 2015). This proves that our BERT-based model is very effective for spatial information extraction.

## Acknowledgments

This research was supported by the AURI (Korea Association of University, Research institute and Industry) grant funded by the Korea Government (MSS: Ministry of SMEs and Startups). (No. S2929950, HRD program for 2020)

## References

Soham Dan, Hangfeng He, and Dan Roth. 2020. Understanding Spatial Relations through Multiple Modalities. *Proceedings of The 12th Language Resources and Evaluation Conference (LREC2020)*. Pages 2368-2372.

Jacob Devlin, Ming-Wei Chang, Kenton Lee, and Kristina Toutanova. 2018. Bert: Pre-training of deep bidirectional transformers for language understanding. *arXiv preprint arXiv: 1810.04805.*

Jennifer D'Souza and Vincent Ng. 2015. UTD: Ensemble-based spatial relation extraction. *Proceedings of the 9th International Workshop on Semantic Evaluation (SemEval 2015).*

ISO (2014), 24617-7:2014(E). Language resource management – Semantic annotation framework – Part 7: Spatial information (ISOspace)

Bogyum Kim and Jae Sung Lee. 2016. Extracting Spatial Entities and Relations in Korean Text. *Proceedings of COLING 2016, the 26th International Conference on Computational Linguistics: Technical Papers.* pages 2389-2396.

Parisa Kordjamshidi, Martijn Van Otterlo, and Marie-Francine Moens. 2011. Spatial role labeling: Towards extraction of spatial relations from natural language. *ACM Transactions on Speech and Language Processing* (TSLP) 8(3): 1-36.

Parisa Kordjamshidi, Taher Rahgooy, Marie-Francine Moens, James Pustejovsky, Umar Manzoor, and Kirk Roberts. 2017. CLEF 2017: Multimodal spatial role labeling task working notes. *CLEF (Working Notes).*

John Lafferty, Andrew McCallum, and Fernando C.N. Pereira. 2001. Conditional random fields: Probabilistic models for segmenting and labeling sequence data. *Proceeding of the 18th International Conference on Machine Learning 2001 (ICML 2001)*, pages 282-289.

Alexey Mazalov, Bruno Martins, and David Matos. 2015. Spatial Role Labeling with Convolutional Neural Networks. *Proceedings of the 9th Workshop on Geographic Information Retrieval.*

Eric Nichols and Fadi Botros. 2015. SpRL-CWW: Spatial relation classification with independent multi-class models. *Proceedings of the 9th International Workshop on Semantic Evaluation (SemEval 2015).*

Jeffery Pennington, Richard Socher, and Christopher D. Manning. 2014. GloVe: Global vectors for word representation. *Proceedings of the 2014 Conference on Empirical Methods in Natural language Processing (EMNLP).* pages 1532-1543. https://portal.acm.org/citation.cfm?id=655813.

Matthew E. Peters, Mark Neumann, Mohit Iyyer, Matt Gardner, Christopher Clark, Kenton Lee, and Luke Zettlemoyer. 2018. Deep contextualized word representation. *arXiv preprint arXiv: 1802.05365.*

James Pustejovsky, Parisa Kordjamshidi, Marie-Francine Moens, Aaron Levine, Seth Dworman, and Zachary Yocum. 2015. Semeval-2015 task 8: Spaceeval. *Proceedings of the 9th International Workshop on Semantic Evaluation (semeval 2015).* pages 884-894.

Alec Radford, Karthik Narasimhan, Tim Salimans, and Ilya Sutskever. 2018. Improving Language Understanding by Generative Pre-Training. *URL* https://s3-us-west-2.amazonaws.com/openai-assets/research-covers/language-unsupervised/language_understanding_paper.pdf

Kirk Roberts and Sanda M. Haragagiu. 2012. UTD-SpRL:A joint approach to spatial role labeling. **SEM 2012: The First Joint Conference on Lexical and Computational Semantics-Volume 1: Proceedings of the main conference and the shared task, and Volume 2: Proceedings of the Sixth International Workshop on Semantic Evaluation (SemEval 2012).* pages 419-424.

Haritz Salaberri, Olatz Arregi, and Beñat Zapirain. 2015. IXAGroupEHUSpaceEval: (X-Space) A WordNet-based approach towards the automatic recognition of spatial information following the ISO-Space annotation scheme. *Proceedings of the 9th International Workshop on Semantic Evaluation (SemEval 2015).*

J.A.K. Suykens and J. Vandewalle. 1999. Least squares support vector machine classifiers. *Neural processing letters* 9(3):293-300.

Ashish Vaswani, Noam Shazeer, Niki Parmar, Jakob Uszkoreit, Llion Jones, Aidan N. Gomez, Łukasz Kaiser, and Illia Polosukhin. 2017. Attention is all you need. *Advances in neural information processing systems.* pages 5998-6008.

Shanchan Wu and Yifan He. 2019. Enriching pre-trained language model with entity information for relation classification. *Proceedings of the 28th ACM International Conference on Information and Knowledge Management.* pages 2361-2364.

Yonghui Wu, Mike Schuster, Zhifeng Chen, Quoc V Le, Mohammad Norouzi, Wolfgang Macherey, Maxim Krikun, Yuan Cao, Qin Gao, Klaus Macherey, Jeff Klingner, Apurva Shah, Melvin Johnson, Xiaobing Liu, Łukasz Kaiser, Stephan Gouws, Yoshikiyo Kato, Taku Kudo, Hideto Kazawa, Keith Stevens, George Kurian, Nishant Patil, Wei Wang, Cliff Young, Jason Smith, Jason Riesa, Alex Rudnick, Oriol Vinyals, Greg Corrado, Macduff Hughes, and Jeffrey Dean. 2016. Google's neural machine translation system: Bridging the gap between human and machine translation. *arXiv preprint arXiv: 1609.08144.*

Zhilin Yang, Zihang Dai, Yiming Yang, Jaime Carbonell, Ruslan Salakhutdinov, and Quoc V. Le. 2019. Xlnet: Generalized autoregressive pretraining for language understanding. *Advances in neural information processing systems.* pages 5753-5763.

Éloi Zablocki, Patrick Bordes, Laure Soulier, Benjamin Piwowarski, and Patrick Gallinari. 2017. LIP6@ CLEF2017: Multi-modal spatial role labeling using word embeddings. *CLEF (Working Notes).*

# A Cognitively Motivated Approach to Spatial Information Extraction

**Chao Xu**
Shandong University / China
chao.xu@sdu.edu.cn

**Dagmar Gromann**
University of Vienna / Austria
dagmar.gromann@univie.ac.at

**Emmanuelle Dietz**
TU Dresden / Germany
emmanuelle.dietz@tu-dresden.de

**Beihai Zhou**
Peking University / China
zhoubh@pku.edu.cn

## Abstract

Automatic extraction of spatial information from natural language can boost human-centered applications that rely on spatial dynamics. The field of cognitive linguistics has provided theories and cognitive models to address this task. Yet, existing solutions tend to focus on specific word classes, subject areas, or machine learning techniques that cannot provide cognitively plausible explanations for their decisions. We propose an automated spatial semantic analysis (ASSA) framework building on grammar and cognitive linguistic theories to identify spatial entities and relations, bringing together methods of spatial information extraction and cognitive frameworks on spatial language. The proposed rule-based and explainable approach contributes constructions and preposition schemas and outperforms previous solutions on the CLEF-2017 standard dataset.

## 1 Introduction

Human-centered technologies, such as in self-driving cars or cognitive assistance systems in aviation, face the challenge of having to provide cognitively plausible decisions, i.e., decisions that are understandable and accepted by humans. This is needed for an effortless interaction between artificial and human agents. Yet, even in spatial language, with its advantageous characteristic of following recurring, uniform patterns (Talmy, 2005), drawing automated inferences in a dynamic spatial environment remains to be an open research question. As illustration consider Example (🥛)[1]: "I poured water from the bottle into the cup until it was full"[2]. Consider the question: "What was full, the cup or the bottle?". A cognitively plausible explanation for the answer *the cup*, could be as follows: "As *water was poured from the bottle into the cup*, it is likely that the water is in the cup. Normally, if *water* is poured into *the cup* then *the cup* is *full*. Thus, there is some evidence that the cup is full." In order to produce and accept "the cup" as the plausible answer, humans do not require particular reasoning effort or expert knowledge. Yet building systems that provide such *simple* explanations remains to be a challenge.

In the past, a considerable amount of literature has been published on automated spatial semantic analysis. However, most of the solutions focus on specific spatial phenomena suffering from a lack of generalizability (e.g. Platonov and Schubert, 2018; Ulinski et al., 2019), or are generalizable machine learning approaches (e.g. Kordjamshidi et al., 2011), but lack explainability of provided decisions. Also cognitive linguistics contributed to the understanding of spatial language by proposing various cognitive models to this end (Jackendoff, 1983; Talmy, 1983).

Taking spatial cognitive models as a starting point, we propose a novel spatial representation method and investigate which type of spatial information, such as entities of spatial scenes and relations holding between them, can be extracted from natural language (NL) expressions. To this end, we rely on construction grammar and cognitive linguistic theories. For Example (🥛), the following spatial roles apply: *agent* ("I"), *figure* ("water"), *ground* ("bottle" and "cup"), and simultaneously *source* ("bottle") and *goal* ("cup").

Figure 1 illustrates the automated spatial semantic analysis (ASSA) framework proposed in this paper. ASSA provides an automated extraction method based on construction grammar and image schemas (Lakoff, 1987; Johnson, 1987), which are spatio-temporal relationships built from sensori-

[1]Instead of numbering examples, we identify them with a unique semantic symbol in brackets.

[2]Adapted from Example 24 in the Winograd Schema Challenge (WSC) dataset https://cs.nyu.edu/faculty/davise/papers/WinogradSchemas/WSCollection.html (24.7.2020)



*Proceedings of the Third International Workshop on Spatial Language Understanding (SpLU 2020)*, pages 18–28
November 19, 2020. 
https://doi.org/10.18653/v1/P17

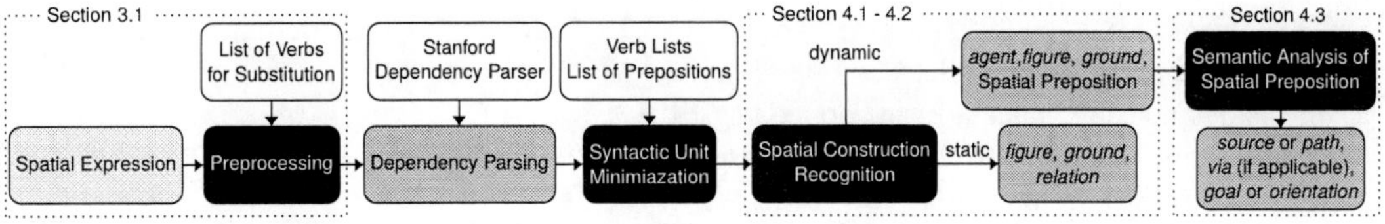


Figure 1: External sources are in white, input/ output are in light gray and own contributions are in black boxes.

motor experiences. Based on theories and analyses of spatial language derived from the Winograd Schema Challenge (WSC) dataset, a list of constructions to parse spatial sentences is derived (Section 3.1). We classify a list of verbs from VerbNet (Schuler, 2005) into dynamic and static, helping the classification of NL statements into dynamic and static constructions (Section 4.2). Prepositions have been found to be supreme spatial indicators in NL (Talmy, 1983; Kordjamshidi et al., 2011), so we encode spatial information of prepositions in what we call preposition schemas (Section 4.3) building on image schemas to help identifying spatial roles and their relations.

To the best of our knowledge, this is the first generalizable and explainable framework grounded in construction grammars and cognitive linguistic theories to be empirically validated. We firmly believe and show that exploiting insights gained from cognitive linguistics can help building such a framework. This framework contributes to the automated analysis of spatial semantics in NL and thereby to the analysis of the human experience of space and human-centered applications. Our contributions are: (1) A semantic analysis of spatial prepositions based on image schemas, (2) An automated extraction method that unifies constructionist theory and cognitive linguistic insights on spatial language, and (3) A prototype system of ASSA fully evaluated on a standardized dataset with competitive performance.

## 2 Related Work

Our work combines two strands of research, namely spatial semantic analysis and (automated) spatial role labeling. Spatial semantic analysis – the process of detecting spatial entities, their relations, and motion – has been a long-standing research endeavor in areas such as cognitive linguistics (e.g. Naidu et al., 2018; Talmy, 1983), geographical information systems (GIS) (e.g. Zhang et al., 2009; Melo and Martins, 2017), spatial language understanding in robotics (e.g. Spranger et al., 2016) as well as spatial role labeling (Kordjamshidi et al., 2011). At times, works focus on one aspect of spatial semantic analysis only, such as prepositions (Platonov and Schubert, 2018) and spatial frames and their relations (Ulinski et al., 2019).

We consider three works as particularly closely related to the proposed framework. First, Spranger et al. (2016) similarly to our work distinguish dynamic and static spatial relations, however, focus on robot-robot interactions. Second, the Embodied Construction Grammar (Bergen and Chang, 2005) brings together construction and cognitive grammar, which is, however, exemplified rather than fully evaluated. Third, Egorova et al. (2018) propose a knowledge-based approach on fictive motion, who rely on cognitive linguistic theories, rules and verbs to differentiate actual motion from fictive motion. However, they focus on fictive motion in the geographic domain, such as "The valley ran towards the sea". Though such methods are good starting points for extracting variations of spatio-temporal information, they are less suited to reconstruct static and dynamic spatial scences from linguistic descriptions, which we propose to do with a generalizable and evaluated analysis framework.

Methods specific to spatial role labeling have mostly utilized machine learning. Kordjamshidi et al. (2011) apply a step-wise approach with two probabilistic classifiers, where the first step consists in uncovering the spatial indicator (a preposition) and the second in extracting the related trajector and landmark. While this machine learning method has a lot to offer, it disregards the influence of verbs as indicators of movement. However, verbs play a central role in identifying the relation between trajector and landmark and represent a vital element of our proposed method.

One approach testing on the same evaluation dataset, the Spatial Role Labeling shared task at CLEF-2017 (Kordjamshidi et al., 2017), is the LIP6 system (Zablocki et al., 2017). They re-implement

Saul (Kordjamshidi et al., 2015) for the two subtasks of identifying spatially-related entities (trajector, spatial indicator, landmark) and organizing them into spatial triplets. To this end, a sparse perceptron classifier is trained for each of these entities, utilizing lexical, syntactical, and contextual features. While the results are partially competitive to ours, this machine learning method requires complex feature engineering and allows for little insight into decisions taken for each entity. In contrast, ASSA is highly transparent and each decision taken can be fully explained based on the linguistic properties of the spatial expression and the assigned constructional schema and cognitive semantic roles.

## 3 Theoretical Foundations

Our approach is based on cognitive linguistic theories, specifically Talmy's cognitive semantic theory, Goldberg's construction grammar, and Lakoff's and Johnson's image schemas.

### 3.1 Talmy's Analysis of Spatial Language

Talmy (1985) introduced the following four semantic elements to characterize a motion event: *motion*, *path*, *figure*, and *ground*. A motion event consists of one object, the *figure*, moving or located w.r.t. another object, the *ground*. The *figure* refers to the entity that draws focal attention, while the *ground* refers to the entity in the periphery of attention. Consider the following sentence: "The cat was lying by the mouse hole" (🐱). The *figure* in (🐱) is "the cat", and the *ground* is "the mouse hole". Usually in English, the manner or the movement of the event is encoded by the verb, whereas the path or the spatial relation, is encoded in the preposition in a spatial expression (Talmy, 2005; Kordjamshidi et al., 2011). Prepositions as spatial indicators and verbs as movement indicators provide an excellent starting point for spatial information extraction.

Talmy lists a number of verbs that encode *path*: "enter, exit, ascend, descend, cross, pass, circle, advance, proceed, approach, arrive, depart, return, join, separate, part, rise, leave, near, follow" (Talmy, 2000b). Some of these verbs can be substituted by a verb-preposition combination with equivalent meaning. For instance, "exit" and "enter" can be substituted by "get out of" and "get into" respectively.

### 3.2 Goldberg's Construction Grammar

In cognitive linguistics, several construction grammars have been proposed, among others, by Fillmore et al. (1988), Goldberg (1995), and Croft (2001). For the ASSA semantic role extraction presented in Section 5, Goldberg's construction grammar was applied. Her approach focuses on the argument structure of sentence-level constructions, such as *caused-motion construction* and *ditransitive construction*. More importantly, it provides the syntactic-semantic interface between semantic roles and argument roles of an argument structure construction. One of its important principles is that the grammar of a language cannot exclusively be represented by a formal system with rules defining well-formed sequences, but rather consists of constructions. A construction is a form-meaning pair, where neither the form nor the meaning can be fully determined by its individual components, i.e., words or phrases, or other previously established constructions. For instance, "I kicked the ball into the room" (⚽), implies '$X$ caused $Y$ to move $Z$' (*caused-motion*), where $X$, $Y$ and $Z$, are associated with "I", "the ball", and "into the room", in (⚽), respectively. *Caused-motion* cannot be generally assigned to "kick". If it could, then "I kicked the heavy stone, but the stone did not move" would imply that "I caused the heavy stone to move, but the stone did not move", which seems unreasonable. However, we can assign the caused-motion to the construction instead.

Goldberg proposed the correspondence principle, in which correspondence describes the relations between the participant roles of the verb and the argument roles of the argument structure construction, e.g. agent, theme, location roles. For the above example, the correspondence relation between participant roles and argument roles is as follows:

| Instance | I | kicked | the ball | into the room |
|---|---|---|---|---|
| Semantic | Agent | Action | Patient | Path |
| Syntactic | NP | VP | NP | PP |
| Grammatical | Subject | Predicate | Object | Complement |

This principle provides a syntactic-semantic interface and indicates that once the construction type of a sentence is identified, we can obtain the corresponding semantic roles of syntactic elements based on their correspondence relations.

### 3.3 Image Schemas

Within the tradition of embodied cognition, image schemas (Johnson, 1987; Lakoff, 1987) are described as spatio-temporal relationships learned from recurring sensorimotor experiences with our environment from early infancy on that through analogical reasoning can be used to explain and predict outcomes on any current or future situation. Image schemas are believed to provide a missing link between physical experiences and high-level cognition, such as language and reasoning. For instance, if a child has learned that it can go IN and OUT of a tent – having learned the image schema of CONTAINMENT – it can transfer this information to other instances of this image schema, such as an eggshell as CONTAINER for egg yolk and white. As discussed in detail in Hedblom et al. (2018), each image schema represents a family of building blocks that can constitute different variants of the basic image schema, such as a lake can be seen as a CONTAINER with a flexible number of openings – the surface can be entered and exited at any point – whereas a tunnel has one opening to enter and one to exit. These building blocks are called spatial primitives, such as IN, OUT and CONTAINER, that compose more complex image schemas and schematic integrations (Mandler and Pagán Cánovas, 2014). For instance, variations of SOURCE_PATH_GOAL compositions could be only SOURCE_PATH or PATH_GOAL. There is no hierarchy for image schemas or the composition of spatial primitives, but in form of integrations various image schemas can come together in one spatial scene or also the lexical description of such a scene. Several spatial primitives resonate of preposition meanings, such as the image schema VERTICALITY being defined by the UP and DOWN that resonate of the prepositions "up" and "down", which represent the basis for the preposition schemas proposed in this paper.

## 4 Spatial Semantic Analysis Framework

The spatial semantic analysis framework covers three components depicted on the right of Figure 1: Section 4.1 specifies the semantic roles, Section 4.2 develops the spatial constructional schemas for the identification of these roles and their relations, and Section 4.3 provides the semantic analysis framework for the proposed preposition schemas.

| Roles | Description |
|---|---|
| *figure* | Entity that needs to be located. |
| *ground* | Reference entity w.r.t. which *figure*'s location is characterized. |
| *relation* | Relative location of *figure* and *ground*. |
| *agent* | Entity that causes *figure* to move. |
| *source* | Location of *figure* before it changes location. |
| *path* | Shape of trajectory of *figure*'s movement. |
| *goal* | location of *figure* after it changes location. |
| *via* | A place on the way of *figure*'s movement. |
| *orientation* | Orientation of *figure*'s movement. |

Table 1: The spatial semantic roles w.r.t. the spatial expression type.

### 4.1 Semantic Roles

Following Talmy's description of a motion event frame in Section 3.1, there are basic semantic roles: *figure* and *ground*. Additionally, spatial expressions can either be dynamic or static. The former describes the motion event, such as for Example (🗑), while the latter describes the state-of-affairs and does not involve movement of entities, such as for Example (🐱). For static spatial expressions, *relation* represents the spatial relations between *figure* and *ground* in Table 1. To characterize the location change in a motion event, the following semantic roles are identified as described in Table 1: *agent*, *source*, *path*, *goal*, *via*, and *orientation*. Here *path* refers to the trajectory of the *figure*'s movement, while *path* in Talmy's theory includes more information such as *source*, *via*, and *goal*, which we model separately from *path*.

### 4.2 Spatial Constructional Schemas

The correspondence principle introduced in Section 3.2 allows us to identify semantic roles by identifying syntactic constructions of spatial NL statements. We propose 7 constructional schemas shown in Table 2 based on a manual analysis of 78 spatial examples of the WSC dataset and 3 further ones from analyzing examples provided in literature (Sondheimer, 1978; Herskovits, 1987)[3]. Dynamic and static spatial statements are distinguished by the dynamic and stative verb in the sentence.

Each construction consists of several basic constituents. Noun phrases (NP), verbs (Verb), and prepositions (Prep) represent grammatical categories that are refined regarding their role in spa-

[3]Note that the validation of those constructions has been performed on an entirely different dataset (see Section 6).

| Type | Index | Constructional Schema |
|---|---|---|
| | D-1 | $NP_F$ - MV - Spatial Prep - $NP_G$ |
| Dynamic | D-2 | $NP_F$ - MV - Spatial Prep |
| Schemas | D-3 | $NP_A$ - CMV - $NP_F$ - Spatial Prep - $NP_G$ |
| | D-4 | $NP_A$ - CMV - $NP_F$ - Spatial Prep |
| | S-1 | There be - $NP_F$ - Spatial Prep - $NP_G$ |
| | S-2 | $NP_F$ - Spatial Prep - $NP_G$ |
| Static | S-3 | $NP_F$ - Be - Spatial Prep - $NP_G$ |
| Schemas | S-4 | Spatial Prep - $NP_G$ - Be - $NP_F$ |
| | S-5 | $NP_F$ - SV - Spatial Prep - $NP_G$ |
| | S-6 | Spatial Prep - $NP_G$ - SV - $NP_F$ |

Table 2: List of constructional schemas, where subscript "F" stands for *figure*, "G" stands for *ground*, and "A" stands for *agent*.

| Relative Prepositions | | | |
|---|---|---|---|
| above | across | after | against |
| ahead of | along | alongside | amid |
| amidst | among | amongst | apart from |
| around | aside | at | atop |
| away from | back | back of | before |
| behind | below | beneath | beside |
| between | betwixt | beyond | but |
| by | close to | down | far from |
| in | in back of | in between | in front of |
| in line with | in place of | in the back of | in the front of |
| in the middle of | in the midst of | inside | inside of |
| left of | near | near to | nearby |
| next to | of | on | on top of |
| opposite | opposite of | outside | outside of |
| over | off | round | throughout |
| to the left of | to the right of | to the side of | toward |
| under | underneath | up | upon |
| within | | | |
| **Dynamic Prepositions** | | | |
| from | into | off | off of |
| on to | onto | out | out of |
| past | through | to | via |

Table 3: List of Spatial Prepositions

tial language. NPs can either represent a *figure* ($NP_F$), a *ground* ($NP_G$), or an *agent* ($NP_A$). We select some verbs that can appear in the constructions listed in Table 2, and classify them into three classes: *motion verbs* (MV), such as "run", *caused motion verbs* (CMV), such as "sweep", or *stative verbs* (SV), such as "lie". The reason that we made such selection is that we try to exclude the non-spatial expressions in some extent by restricting the verbs, e.g., if there is no restriction on verbs, "I cut the meat into pieces" will be misrecognized as conforming to the constructional schema D-3, but it is not a motion construction. A caused motion is triggered by external force, whereas a motion exists without an external force. To further foster correct classification we treat occurrences of "to be" without any other verbs and "there is/are" as stative. The final constituent of constructional schemas are prepositions, which in the case of spatial language per definition are classified as spatial.

A verb can belong to different verb classes: *move* belongs to both, the motion verb class and the caused motion verb class, as the following examples show: *I* ($NP_F$) *move* (MV) *into* (Prep) *the new house* ($NP_G$) shows a dynamic construction where *move* functions as a motion verb. Yet, *I* ($NP_A$) *move* (CMV) *the box* ($NP_F$) *into* (Prep) *the room* ($NP_G$) uses the same verb as a caused motion verb. The function in the sentence determines which type of motion is being referred to. Static constructions, on the other hand, specify the static relative location of different entities. Based on these constructions we specify three general principles to identify spatial roles: (i) in a nonagentive clause, the subject and object function as *figure* and *ground* respectively; (ii) in an agentive clause, subject, direct object, and indirect object function as *agent*, *figure*, and *ground* respectively (Talmy, 2000a); (iii) a *ground* always appears after a spatial preposition. We empirically validated these principles as described below that guide our constructional schemas. The schemas in Table 2 are then utilized to recognize types and roles in linguistic expressions. These are uniquely recognized w.r.t. the syntactic structure of the spatial expression as exemplified in Section 5 (Step 4).

### 4.3 Semantic Analysis of Spatial Prepositions

Spatial information is frequently encoded in spatial prepositions (Section 3.1). This section describes the contribution of prepositions to spatial role identification.

**Spatial Prepositions**: A spatial preposition describes the location of an entity in relation to other entities. An advantage of closed-class elements and in particular prepositions is their rather limited inventory with limited options to increase their number as opposed to other word classes. We present a fairly complete list of prepositions in Table 3 that was taken from Landau and Jackendoff (1993); Quirk et al. (2010); Dittrich et al. (2015).[4]

Spatial prepositions can be divided into two gen-

[4]There are some variations in classifications that we do not consider here: According to Landau and Jackendoff (1993) adverbs, such as *backward* and *forward*, are intransitive prepositions; Dittrich et al. (2015) classify phrases such as *west of* as prepositions.

eral types depending on the constructions in which they appear: relative prepositions and dynamic prepositions. Relative prepositions are the ones that spatially relate two or more entities, and can be used in both dynamic and static constructions. Dynamic prepositions co-occur with movement and are frequently used in dynamic constructions.

The reason we made such distinction is to distinguish Example (🥛) from: "I poured water from the bottle on the table". In this example, the corresponding *figure* of 'on the table' is 'the bottle' rather than 'water', while the *figure* of 'into the cup' is 'water' rather than 'the bottle' in Example (🥛). For the example, the first part (i.e., "I poured water from the bottle") should be recognized by dynamic constructional schema D-3, and the second part (i.e., "the bottle on the table") should be recognized by the static constructional schema S-2 in Table 2. These two examples mainly differ in their use of prepositions, namely *into* and *on*. Given a spatial expression, if its first part is recognized by a dynamic construction, and the preposition phrase (PP) after the first part describes a movement, namely using dynamic prepositions, then the *figure* of this PP is the same as the *figure* of the first part, and further roles are determined according to Table 4. Otherwise, this PP and the NP before it are recognized by another constructional schema.

**Image Schemas and Semantic Analysis:** Following Section 3.3, we assume that spatial primitives of image schemas can help understand and classify spatial prepositions. Figure 2 depicts a number of spatial primitives to characterize spatial relations expressed by prepositions. These schemas are utilized to identify corresponding semantic roles of spatial prepositions, and most of them come from the previous research on image schema and semantic analysis of prepositions such as Johnson (1987); Herskovits (1987); Coventry and Garrod (2004).

For instance, the INTO primitive describes the dynamic spatial relation of an entity in relation to a CONTAINER. Furthermore, it describes a dynamic process of an entity moving from the exterior of a CONTAINER via an opening to the interior of the CONTAINER. This primitive characterizes the spatial relation expressed by the prepositions "into", "in", and "inside of". Movement always requires the change of location, which links it naturally to a SOURCE_PATH_GOAL image schema. In Table 4, we map the spatial primitives of this schema – *source*, *via*, and *goal*, which also correspond to

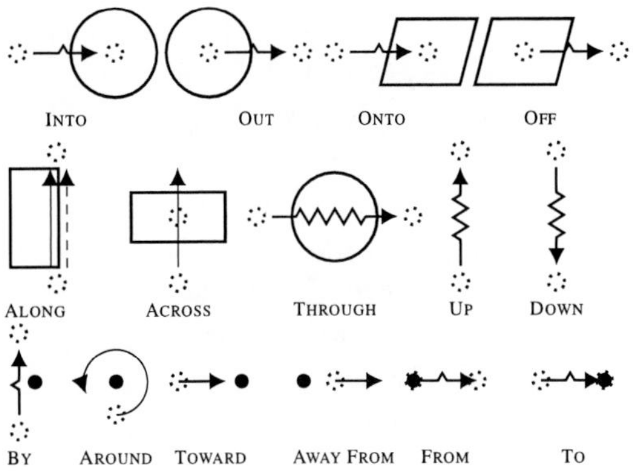


Figure 2: Diagrams for spatial primitives of spatial prepositions

| Preposition | Source | Via | Goal |
|---|---|---|---|
| in, into, inside | exterior | opening | interior |
| out, out of | interior | opening | exterior |
| on, onto | - | - | surface |
| off, off of | surface | - | - |
| from | ground | - | - |
| to | - | - | ground |
| across,through | one side | points(inside) | the other side |
| up, upon | lower place | - | upper place |
| down | higher place | - | lower place |
| by | - | points(near) | - |
| **Preposition** | **Path** | **Via** | **Orientation** |
| along | line | points(inside, near) | - |
| around | arc | points(near) | - |
| toward | - | - | toward |
| away from | - | - | away from |

Table 4: Semantic analysis of spatial prepositions

semantic roles – to the elements of the respective type of movement indicated by the preposition. For the CONTAINER the type of movement relates to its spatial primitives, that is, the exterior, interior, boundary, and opening. Other image schemas, such as a more relative SUPPORT schema as in "the bottle on the table", can be analyzed utilizing the relative propositions presented in Table 4.

## 5 Procedure of ASSA

We describe the procedure of ASSA for our empirical validation of the proposed framework in Section 4. Our prototype system is written in Python and utilizes the Stanford Dependency Parser (Manning et al., 2014). Figure 1 depicts the process, where the following steps will be detailed here:

1. **Preprocessing** If the spatial expression contains a verb that encodes *path* information,

the verb is substituted by a synonymous verb+preposition. For instance, "exit" is replaced by "get out of" to enable the spatial preposition analysis. (Section 3.1).

2. **Dependency parsing** Utilizing the Stanford Dependency Parser (Chen and Manning, 2014), a parse tree is constructed.
3. **Syntactic Unit Minimization** Spliting sentence into syntactic units, or merging neighboring words into a syntactic unit.
4. **Spatial Construction Recognition** Identifying corresponding constructional schema by fuzzy pattern match, and extracting semantic roles: *agent*, *figure*, *ground*, and *relation*.
5. **Semantic Analysis of Spatial Preposition** For dynamic spatial language, indentifying spatial roles by analyzing the spatial prepositions.

As illustration, let us consider the first part of (🥛): "I poured water from the bottle into the cup" (🥃). After Step 1, nothing has changed for 🥃, i.e., 🥃' = 🥃, as no verb that encodes *path* information appears in this example.

In Step 2, we generate a dependency tree and label words with their Part-of-Speech (POS) tags. The following dependency graph shows the result of Step 2:

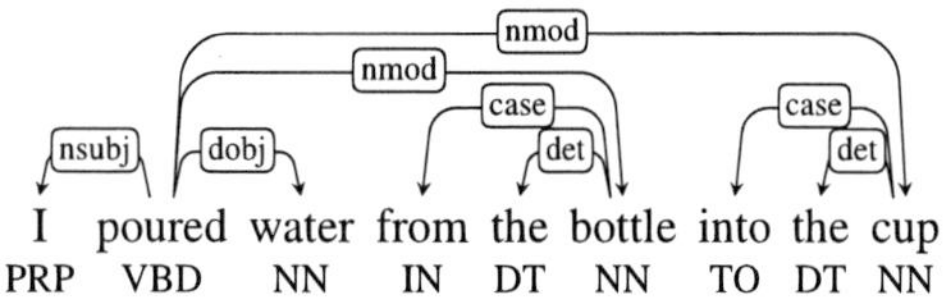


In Step 3, we utilize dependency relations, such as `det` for determiner, to chunk words into syntactic units, e.g. "the bottle" and "the cup" in 🥃'. It is worth noting that in the above dependency tree, the prepositions "from" and "to" are labeled with different POS tags, namely, "IN" and "TO" respectively. So in order to maintain consistency of the annotation of spatial prepositions, we labeled the prepositions in Table 3 with the POS tag "RP". Additionally, each of these prepositions is treated as a single syntactic unit.

To guide the constructional schema identification, a list of verbs from VerbNet (Schuler, 2005) has been classified by two people into motion verb (MV), caused-motion verb (CMV), and stative verb (SV). For these three kinds of verbs, we use MV, CMV, or SV as their POS tags, replacing the original tags generated from Stanford dependency parser. The result of Step 3 is as follows:

| I | poured | water | from | the bottle | into | the cup |
|---|---|---|---|---|---|---|
| PRP | CMV | NN | RP | NN | RP | NN |

In Step 4, we use several fuzzy patterns to recognize the corresponding constructional schemas of spatial expressions, which are listed in Table 2. In general, each constructional schema corresponds to a fuzzy pattern[5]. For instance, the fuzzy pattern [[NN, NNS, NNP, NNPS, PRP, WP], [3], [CMV], [3], [NN, NNS, NNP, NNPS, PRP], [3], [RP], [2], [NN, NNS, NNP, NNPS, PRP]] is used to recognize the dynamic construction D-3 in Table 2,

$$NP_A \text{ - CMV - } NP_F \text{ - Spat Prep - } NP_G. \quad (\text{Con}(🥃'))$$

The numbers in the pattern, such as "[3]", can be replaced with less than 3 elements of any other POS tags such as "MD (modal auxiliary)", "RB (adverb)". It is worth mentioning that the fuzzy patterns only captures the syntactic features of the constructional schemas. Depending on the syntactic-semantic correspondence relation shown in constructional schemas, we could obtain the semantic roles *agent*, *figure*, *ground*, and *relation*.

For the example 🥃', it's syntactic feature could be represented as follows: [[PRP], [CMV], [NN], [RP], [NN], [RP], [NN]], which has been obtained in Step 3. It could be matched by the corresponding fuzzy pattern of constructional schema Con(🥃'). The match algorithm could be understood as a simpler regular expression match, but it works on the word level rather than the character level. According to the syntactic-semantic correspondence relations, "I" and "water" are identified as *agent* and *figure*, respectively, and "the bottle" and "the cup" as *ground*.

In Step 5, we extract spatial roles by analyzing the semantics of spatial prepositions. Given Con(🥃'), the spatial prepositions, "from" and "to" in (🥃) belong respectively to the FROM and INTO schemas in Table 4. According to FROM schema, we could identify the "the bottle" as the *source* of the *figure* "water". Similarly, we could obtain that *source*, *via*, and *goal* of the *figure* "water" are "the exterior of the cup", "the opening of the cup", and "the interior of the cup" respectively by analyzing INTO schema. Up to now, we have obtained all spatial

[5]A full list of constructions and the algorithm can be found here: `https://github.com/chaoxu95/emnlp2020-code/blob/master/fuzzy_match.py`

| Automated Spatial Semantic Analysis (ASSA) | | | | | | Baseline | | | | | LIP6 System | | | | |
|---|---|---|---|---|---|---|---|---|---|---|---|---|---|---|---|
| | Subtask 1 | | | | Subtask 2 | Subtask 1 | | | | Subtask 2 | Subtask 1 | | | | Subtask 2 |
| | SP | TR | LM | Overall | Relation | SP | TR | LM | Overall | Relation | SP | TR | LM | Overall | Relation |
| **Precision** | 94.43 | 71.01 | 84.52 | 82.77 | 60.26 | 94.76 | 56.72 | 72.97 | 75.36 | 75.18 | 97.59 | 79.29 | 94.05 | 89.55 | 68.33 |
| **Recall** | 83.15 | 75.40 | 82.90 | 80.06 | 64.43 | 97.74 | 69.56 | 86.21 | 83.81 | 45.47 | 61.13 | 53.43 | 60.73 | 58.03 | 48.03 |
| **F1** | 88.43 | 73.14 | 83.70 | 81.26 | 62.28 | 96.22 | 62.49 | 79.04 | 78.68 | 56.67 | 75.17 | 63.84 | 73.81 | 70.41 | 56.41 |
| **LCount** | 795 | 874 | 573 | 2242 | 939 | - | - | - | - | - | 795 | 874 | 573 | 2242 | 939 |
| **PCount** | 700 | 928 | 562 | 2190 | 1004 | - | - | - | - | - | 498 | 589 | 370 | 1457 | 660 |

Table 5: Overview of the performance of ASSA compared to the two state-of-the-art systems.

roles in the example (⊔). The implementation of ASSA can be found at `https://github.com/chaoxu95/emnlp2020-code`.

The extracted output after the application of ASSA on a spatial expression gives us insights about the expression's type of verbs, figures and grounds. We believe that these are necessary ingredients for integrating background knowledge within commonsense (spatial) reasoning systems to provide cognitively plausible explanations on the environments' change. Providing full NL explanations of our system's decisions based on presented ingredients is part of our future endeavors.

## 6 Evaluation

We are not aware of any specific shared task as a suitable evaluation for the novel approach proposed here. Spatial role labeling (SpRL), a subtask of SemEval (Kordjamshidi et al., 2012) seems to be the closest related task for our purpose.

We use the test data from the SpRL task of CLEF-2017 to test the coverage of our system. It has 3 subtasks: (1) label spatial indicators and their landmark(s)/trajector(s), (2) extract triplets of spatial indicator-trajector-landmark, (3) label relations with region, direction and distance. Only the first two are relevant for the evaluation of our framework[6]. Consider the following example: *About 20 kids in traditional clothing and hats waiting on stairs.* For Subtask 1 this means identifying the trajector *kids*, spatial indicator *on* and landmark as *stairs*. For Subtask 2 the system should extract *spatial_relation(kids, on, stairs)*.

### 6.1 Datasets and Results

The training set and test set in the SpRL dataset has 600 and 613 sentences respectively. As ASSA is based on linguistic theories and fuzzy matching, no training is required. However, as our underlying assumptions for the representation differs from the test standard in the SpRL task, the training set was utilized to adapt our prototype to this task.

The main change is representing "on the left" and "on the right". In the human-annotated corpus, these two phrases are recognized as the *spatial indicator*, whereas, in our system, "on" is recognized as the *spatial indicator*, while "the right" and "the left" are recognized as *ground*. There are 32 such phrases in the training data and 190 in the test data, which affected the final result. We added a new construction (S-7), $NP_F$ ["on the left", "on the right"], to account for these cases.

Two systems were available for comparing the performance of ASSA, both relied on machine learning methods: (1) baseline system (Kordjamshidi et al., 2017) identified the single roles and triples by creating classifiers that used lexical, syntactical, contextual, and relational features, and (2) LIP6 system (Zablocki et al., 2017), based on a joint approach allowing for a rich feature set based on the complete relation.

Table 5 shows that our system outperforms the others on F1 score in Subtask 1 and 2, and recall in Subtask 2. SP, TR, LM refer to spatial indicator (*relation*), trajector (*figure*), landmark (*ground*) and Overall to a weighted average of these three values. LCount and PCount refer to the number of labels in the human-annotated corpus and that in the test data. Here, Overall represents their sum.

### 6.2 Discussion

While our approach is computationally simple yet theoretically well grounded and contributes constructional as well as preposition schemas, it still achieves a competitive performance. However, the precision of the LIP6 system is $\sim 8\%$ higher than ASSA. One reason is that the annotation of LIP6 has a higher consistency with the human-annotated

[6]The task description can be found at `https://www.cs.york.ac.uk/semeval-2012/task3/index.html` and CLEFLabs of the Evaluation Forum: More information can be found at `http://www.cs.tulane.edu/~pkordjam/mSpRL_CLEF_lab.htm`

dataset because of the training data. LIP6 uses the *indicators* constructed from training, while we take general spatial prepositions in Table 3 as indicators. An important factor that affects the precision is the treatment for the dressing descriptions. Consider the following text: "One man in a white T-shirt , grey pants and a white cap is holding a shovel"[7]. The relations (one man, in, a white t-shirt), (one man, in, grey pants), (one man, in, a white cap) are recognized by ASSA, but they do not appear in the human-annotated dataset. It seems reasonable to regard them as spatial relations. Another reason for higher precision of LIP6 is that it used the joint approach in Roberts and Harabagiu (2012), which allows for a rich feature set to reach higher precision, but it also causes lower recall. The constructions used by ASSA have been developed by us through an analysis of the Winograd Schema Challenge dataset and from the literature to recognize spatial structures. Precision and recall might be improved by adding more constructions.

ASSA has the following advantages w.r.t. the other systems: (i) for each error, a cognitively plausible explanation of the wrong result can be provided. Because of its symbolic representation, this allows us to track, understand and correct the error. (ii) ASSA can deal with dynamic expressions, and identify the roles such as *source*, *goal*. (iii) ASSA can provide a statistical distribution of types of spatial expressions, e.g., 11%, 59.3%, and 23.2% spatial expressions in the test data are respectively recognized by schemas S-1, S-2, and S-7 in Table 2.

It is worth mentioning that SpRL task is insufficient to evaluate the overall performance of ASSA, as it can not be used to evaluate how successful is ASSA at identifying the semantic roles such as *source*, *via*, and *goal*. Up to now, we have only tested it on a small number of spatial expressions extracted from WSC. The test result could be found at `https://github.com/chaoxu95/emnlp2020-code/blob/master/paper-related/wsc_output`

## 7 Conclusion

Although the extraction of spatial information has been widely studied, no general and human understandable approach has been proposed up to this point. Based on its interdisciplinary nature by exploiting the developments made in various areas, our contributions are two-fold: ASSA unifies methods from automated spatial information extraction with cognitive models on spatial language. The constructional schemas developed here can extract relevant spatial information, and further (in case of a dynamic construction) apply them to image schemas in order to identify corresponding semantic roles. Second, an evaluation of a prototype system outperforms machine learning systems. In terms of future work, it would be interesting to apply the prototype to a larger dataset with more dynamic spatial expressions as well as test the procedure on different languages. As discussed above, it would also be interesting to utilize the insights gained from our constructions and preposition schemas to provide natural language explanations for system decisions.

Finally, it would be interesting to investigate the interaction of ASSA with existing resources, such as FrameNet (Baker et al., 1998) to further improve on its precision and provide background knowledge to our framework. It would also be interesting to formally represent our constructional schemas, e.g. utilizing Qualitative Trajectory Calculus (Van de Weghe et al., 2005) and similar formalisms, in order to benefit from reasoning algorithms for spatial information extraction.

[7]Corresponding image: images/00/116.jpg

## Acknowledgments

The first author is supported by the fundamental research funds of Shandong University.

## References

Collin F. Baker, Charles J. Fillmore, and John B. Lowe. 1998. The berkeley framenet project. In *Proceedings of the 36th Annual Meeting of the Association for Computational Linguistics and 17th International Conference on Computational Linguistics - Volume 1*, page 86–90, USA. Association for Computational Linguistics.

Bergen K. Bergen and Nancy Chang. 2005. Embodied construction grammar in simulation-based language understanding. In *Construction grammars: Cognitive grounding and theoretical extensions*, pages 147–190. John Benjamins Publishing Company.

Danqi Chen and Christopher D. Manning. 2014. A fast and accurate dependency parser using neural networks. In *Proceedings of the conference on empirical methods in natural language processing (EMNLP)*, pages 740–750. Association for Computational Linguistics.

Kenny R. Coventry and Simon C. Garrod. 2004. *Seeing, Saying and Acting: The psychological semantics of spatial prepositions*. Psychology Press.

William Croft. 2001. *Radical construction grammar: Syntactic theory in typological perspective*. Oxford University Press.

André Dittrich, Maria Vasardani, Stephan Winter, Timothy Baldwin, and Fei Liu. 2015. A classification schema for fast disambiguation of spatial prepositions. In *Proceedings of the 6th ACM SIGSPATIAL International Workshop on GeoStreaming*, pages 78–86. Association for Computing Machinery.

Ekaterina Egorova, Ludovic Moncla, Mauro Gaio, Christophe Claramunt, and Ross S Purves. 2018. Fictive motion extraction and classification. *International Journal of Geographical Information Science*, 32(11):2247–2271.

Charles J. Fillmore, Paul Kay, and Mary Catherine O'connor. 1988. Regularity and idiomaticity in grammatical constructions: The case of let alone. *Language*, pages 501–538.

Adele E. Goldberg. 1995. *Constructions: A construction grammar approach to argument structure*. University of Chicago Press.

Maria M. Hedblom, Dagmar Gromann, and Oliver Kutz. 2018. In, out and through: formalising some dynamic aspects of the image schema containment. In *Proceedings of the 33rd Annual ACM Symposium on Applied Computing*, pages 918–925. Association for Computing Machinery.

Annette Herskovits. 1987. *Language and spatial cognition: an interdisciplinary study of prepositions in English*. Cambridge University Press.

Ray Jackendoff. 1983. *Semantics and cognition*. MIT press.

Mark Johnson. 1987. *The body in the mind: The bodily basis of meaning, imagination, and reason*. University of Chicago Press.

Parisa Kordjamshidi, Steven Bethard, and Marie-Francine Moens. 2012. Semeval-2012 task 3: Spatial role labeling. In *Proceedings of the First Joint Conference on Lexical and Computational Semantics-Volume 1: Proceedings of the main conference and the shared task, and Volume 2: Proceedings of the Sixth International Workshop on Semantic Evaluation*, pages 365–373. Association for Computational Linguistics.

Parisa Kordjamshidi, Taher Rahgooy, Marie-Francine Moens, James Pustejovsky, Umar Manzoor, and Kirk Roberts. 2017. Clef 2017: Multimodal spatial role labeling (msprl) task overview. In *International Conference of the Cross-Language Evaluation Forum for European Languages*, pages 367–376. Springer.

Parisa Kordjamshidi, Dan Roth, and Hao Wu. 2015. Saul: Towards declarative learning based programming. In *Proceedings of the 24th International Joint Conference on Artificial Intelligence*, volume 2015, pages 1844–1851. AAAI Press.

Parisa Kordjamshidi, Martijn Van Otterlo, and Marie-Francine Moens. 2011. Spatial role labeling: Towards extraction of spatial relations from natural language. *ACM Transactions on Speech and Language Processing*, 8(3):4:1–36.

George Lakoff. 1987. *Women, Fire, and Dangerous Things. What Categories Reveal about the Mind*. The University of Chicago Press.

Barbara Landau and Ray Jackendoff. 1993. "what" and "where" in spatial language and spatial cognition. *Behavioral and brain sciences*, 16(2):217–238.

Jean M. Mandler and Cristóbal Pagán Cánovas. 2014. On defining image schemas. *Language and Cognition*, pages 1–23.

Christopher Manning, Mihai Surdeanu, John Bauer, Jenny Finkel, Steven Bethard, and David McClosky. 2014. The Stanford CoreNLP natural language processing toolkit. In *Association for Computational Linguistics (ACL) System Demonstrations*, pages 55–60.

Fernando Melo and Bruno Martins. 2017. Automated geocoding of textual documents: A survey of current approaches. *Transactions in GIS*, 21(1):3–38.

Viswanatha Naidu, Jordan Zlatev, Vasanta Duggirala, Joost Van De Weijer, Simon Devylder, and Johan Blomberg. 2018. Holistic spatial semantics and post-talmian motion event typology: A case study of thai and telugu. *Cognitive Semiotics*, 11(2):1–27.

Georgiy Platonov and Lenhart Schubert. 2018. Computational models for spatial prepositions. In *Proceedings of the First International Workshop on Spatial Language Understanding*, pages 21–30.

Randolph Quirk, Sidney Greenbaum, Geoffrey Leech, and Jan Svartvik. 2010. *A comprehensive grammar of the English language*. Pearson Education India.

Kirk Roberts and Sanda M Harabagiu. 2012. Utd-sprl: A joint approach to spatial role labeling. In *Proceedings of the First Joint Conference on Lexical and Computational Semantics*, pages 419–424. Association for Computational Linguistics.

Karin Kipper Schuler. 2005. *Verbnet: A Broad-coverage, Comprehensive Verb Lexicon*. Ph.D. thesis, University of Pennsylvania, Philadelphia, PA, USA. AAI3179808.

Norman K. Sondheimer. 1978. A semantic analysis of reference to spatial properties. *Linguistics and Philosophy*, 2(2):235–280.

Michael Spranger, Jakob Suchan, and Mehul Bhatt. 2016. Robust natural language processing: Combining reasoning, cognitive semantics, and construction grammar for spatial language. In *Proceedings of the 25th International Joint Conference on Artificial Intelligence*, pages 2908–2914. AAAI Press.

Leonard Talmy. 1983. How language structures space. In *Spatial orientation*, pages 225–282. Springer.

Leonard Talmy. 1985. Lexicalization patterns: Semantic structure in lexical forms. *Language typology and syntactic description*, 3(99):36–149.

Leonard Talmy. 2000a. *Toward a Cognitive Semantics: Concept Structuring Systems*, volume 1. MIT press.

Leonard Talmy. 2000b. *Toward a Cognitive Semantics: Typology and process*, volume 2. MIT press.

Leonard Talmy. 2005. The fundamental system of spatial schemas in language. In B. Hampe and J. E. Grady, editors, *From perception to meaning: Image schemas in cognitive linguistics*, volume 29 of *Cognitive Linguistics Research*, pages 199–234. Mouton de Gruyter.

Morgan Ulinski, Bob Coyne, and Julia Hirschberg. 2019. Spatialnet: A declarative resource for spatial relations. In *Proceedings of the Combined Workshop on Spatial Language Understanding (SpLU) and Grounded Communication for Robotics (RoboNLP)*, pages 61–70. Association for Computational Linguistics.

Nico Van de Weghe, Bart Kuijpers, Peter Bogaert, and Philippe De Maeyer. 2005. A qualitative trajectory calculus and the composition of its relations. In *International Conference on GeoSpatial Sematics*, pages 60–76. Springer.

Eloi Zablocki, Patrick Bordes, Laure Soulier, Benjamin Piwowarski, and Patrick Gallinari. 2017. Lip6@clef2017: Multi-modal spatial role labeling using word embeddings. In *Working Notes of CLEF 2017-Conference and Labs of the Evaluation Forum*.

Chunjun Zhang, Xueying Zhang, Wenming Jiang, Qijun Shen, and Shanqi Zhang. 2009. Rule-based extraction of spatial relations in natural language text. In *2009 International Conference on Computational Intelligence and Software Engineering*, pages 1–4. IEEE.

# They Are Not All Alike: Answering Different Spatial Questions Requires Different Grounding Strategies

**Alberto Testoni**[1], **Claudio Greco**[1], **Tobias Bianchi**[3], **Mauricio Mazuecos**[2], **Agata Marcante**[4], **Luciana Benotti**[2], **Raffaella Bernardi**[1]

[1] University of Trento, Italy [2] Universidad de Córdoba, Conicet Argentina
[3] ISAE-Supaero, France [4] Université de Lorraine, France

{alberto.testoni|claudio.greco|raffaella.bernardi}@unitn.it
{mmazuecos|luciana.benotti}@unc.edu.ar
tobias.bianchi@student.isae-supaero.fr
agata.marcante7@etu.univ-lorraine.fr

## Abstract

In this paper, we study the grounding skills required to answer spatial questions asked by humans while playing the GuessWhat?! game. We propose a classification for spatial questions dividing them into absolute, relational, and group questions. We build a new answerer model based on the LXMERT multimodal transformer and we compare a baseline with and without visual features of the scene. We are interested in studying how the attention mechanisms of LXMERT are used to answer spatial questions since they require putting attention on more than one region simultaneously and spotting the relation holding among them. We show that our proposed model outperforms the baseline by a large extent (9.70% on spatial questions and 6.27% overall). By analyzing LXMERT errors and its attention mechanisms, we find that our classification helps to gain a better understanding of the skills required to answer different spatial questions.

## 1 Introduction

Visual Dialogues are a useful testbed to study how models ground natural language and in particular how they ground spatial language, which is the focus of our analysis. Visual Dialogues have been the aim of early work on natural language understanding (NLU) (Winograd, 1972) and are now studied by a very active community at the interplay between computer vision and computational linguistics (e.g. Baldridge et al. (2018); Ilinykh et al. (2019); Haber et al. (2019)). Recently, important progress has been made on visual dialogue systems thanks to the release of datasets like VisDial (Das et al., 2017) and GuessWhat?! (de Vries et al., 2017). The former contains chit-chat conversations about an image whereas the latter is a visual game, hence its dialogues are goal-oriented. In both cases, one agent asks questions and the

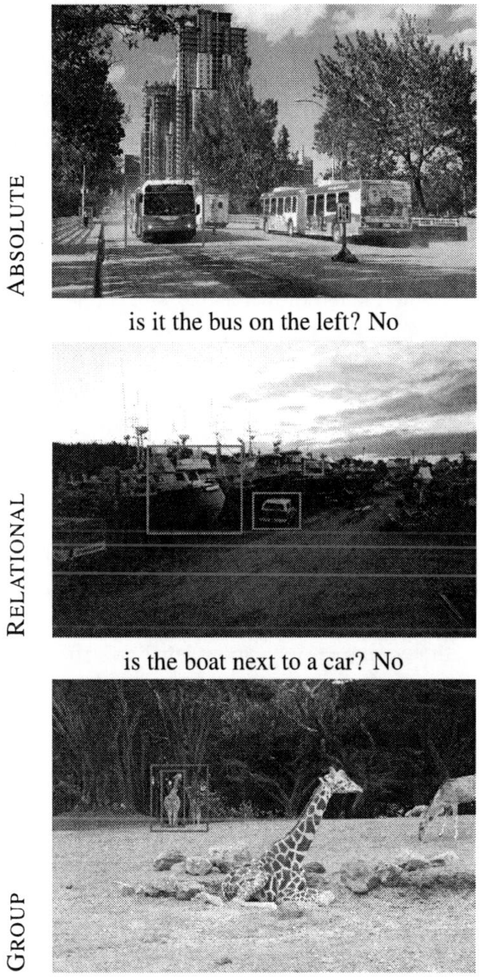


is one of the two in the back? Yes

Figure 1: A vast amount of questions asked by humans in the GuessWhat?! game (de Vries et al., 2017) are spatial. We classify them as *absolute*, *relational*, and *group* based on how they many objects are involved and how they are related. The red box marks the object(s) involved in the question, while the green box marks the target of the game. *Relational* and *group* questions need more than one object, whereas absolute do not.



*Proceedings of the Third International Workshop on Spatial Language Understanding (SpLU 2020)*, pages 29–38
November 19, 2020. 
https://doi.org/10.18653/v1/P17

other, which we call the Oracle, answers. For VisDial most of the work focused on the answerer, but in-depth evaluation has been carried out on the questioner too (eg., Murahari et al. (2019); Testoni et al. (2019)). For GuessWhat?!, instead, work has been done mostly, if not only, on the questioner. Current models trained with reinforcement learning achieve high task success; they adapt to the oracle limitations and end-up asking questions that are linguistically simpler than those asked by humans (Shekhar et al., 2019; Pang and Wang, 2020).

It is interesting to understand where current multimodal NLU models stand with respect to this task: answering questions asked by humans in a goal oriented visual dialogue. Our paper addresses this question by evaluating how the Oracle model of the GuessWhat?! game answers questions asked by humans while playing the game.

GuessWhat?! is a cooperative game where two players talk in order to identify an object in an image. The player known as the *Questioner* has to guess the target by asking yes/no questions. The other player, the *Oracle*, knows the target object and answers the questions. Shekhar et al. (2019) show that most of the questions in the dataset are about the entity of the target ("Is it a female?") or its location ("is it the first one?"). Mazuecos et al. (2020) show that the baseline model, commonly used for the Guesswhat?! task since its introduction in de Vries et al. (2017), has almost human-like accuracy on the entity questions and a much lower accuracy on questions about attributes. In this paper, we focus on spatial questions and classify them into three groups: *absolute*, *relational*, and *group* questions as illustrated in Figure 1.

An unpleasant aspect of the baseline model is that it receives the gold standard entity of the target (that is, the category label, e.g. "giraffe" or "boat") as input. Furthermore, it answers questions without seeing either the image or the visual features of the target, but instead it simply relies on the category label of the target and its coordinates. Important progress on multimodal encoders has been obtained since the GuessWhat?! release; hence, we study the effect of using models that ground the question into the image and do not have access to the gold standard category label of the target. We adapt a multimodal universal encoder, LXMERT (Tan and Bansal, 2019), to play the role of the Oracle and compare it with the baseline model.

It is known that grounding spatial expressions is challenging for neural networks since quite often they require models to put attention on more regions simultaneously and spot the relation holding among them (e.g., the car and the boat in Figure 1, middle). LXMERT is a transformer-based neural network and as such it heavily exploits attention-based mechanisms. In this paper, we run a qualitative analysis of the attention LXMERT exhibits for the different types of location questions and run an in-depth error analysis of its results. To sum up, we make the following contributions:

- We adapt LXMERT to play the role of the Oracle of the GuessWhat?! game obtaining an overall accuracy of 82.21%, an increase of 6.27% with respect to the usual baseline.
- We find that LXMERT improves over the baseline also on spatial questions (+9.70%), but they remain a large source of errors also for this model – with 77.00% accuracy.
- We classify spatial questions into three subtypes and use this classification to annotate the subset of spatial questions in the GuessWhat?! test set. The fine-grained evaluation shows that the hardest spatial questions are the *relational* and *group* ones.
- We run an in-depth qualitative analysis of LXMERT cross-modal attention and an analysis of its errors on each question sub-type. The analysis shows that LXMERT attention differs between *absolute* and *relational* questions as expected, and that some spatial questions need the dialogue history to be interpreted correctly.

The paper proceeds as follows. Section 2 reviews previous work on visual question answering and on spatial referring expressions. Section 3 presents the models providing information on how we adapt LXMERT for the Oracle task. Section 4 describes the dataset and our classification of spatial questions. In Section 5 we compare the accuracy of the models reporting a fine-grained evaluation by question type and zoom into the subset of spatial questions. We further analysed this subset through a manual inspection of LXMERT attention and errors in Section 6, before drawing our conclusions in Section 7. The code of our work is available at: `https://github.com/albertotestoni/unitn_unc_splu2020`.

## 2 Related Work

Answering visual questions is a task that has received increasing attention during the last years. Interesting exploratory analysis has been carried out to understand Visual Question Answering (VQA) systems which highlight their weaknesses and strengths, e.g. (Johnson et al., 2017; Shekhar et al., 2017; Suhr et al., 2017; Kafle and Kanan, 2017). VQA datasets contain both wh- and Y/N-questions. But the kind of Y/N visual questions the Oracle needs to answer are different than those of the VQA datasets: it has to check whether the target has or does not have the questioned property. Hence, it has to compare the target's properties with those of the entity the question refers to and answer accordingly. Moreover, differently from VQA, the GuessWhat?! dataset has been collected in a more naturalistic environment, by letting humans play the games. We adapt LXMERT (Tan and Bansal, 2019), a multimodal universal encoder State-of-the-Art in VQA, to accomplish the Oracle's challenge.

After the introduction of the supervised baseline models (de Vries et al., 2017), several models have been proposed for the Questioner, which are mostly based on reinforcement learning (Sang-Woo et al., 2019; Zhang et al., 2018b; Zhao and Tresp, 2018; Zhang et al., 2018a; Gan et al., 2019; Yang et al., 2019; Pang and Wang, 2020). For these models, the role of the Oracle is even more salient than for models based on supervised or cooperative learning (Shekhar et al., 2019) since they are reinforced to ask those questions the Oracle is good at answering. Despite this important role of the Oracle, no work has been carried out to evaluate and improve it. We aim to fill this gap.

Shekhar et al. (2019) show that GuessWhat?! human players ask quite a lot spatial questions. It has been observed that capturing the spatial relation about objects is challenging for neural network models. Kelleher and Dobnik (2017) argue that Convolutional Neural Network (CNN) do not ground spatial information properly: since they discard location information through the pooling mechanism, their embeddings can only capture rough relative positions of objects within a scene. In line with this claim, Collell and Moens (2018) show that linguistic features are more spatially informative than CNN visual features. New multimodal models, like LXMERT, start from positional aware embeddings. We therefore study how well they handle the spatial questions asked by GuessWhat?! players.

Spatial expressions have been deeply studied within the referring expression generation community. In this area, earlier work (Paraboni et al., 2007) has suggested that, in ordered domains (e.g., a document divided into sections and subsections), referring expressions that include spatial information, even when redundant, lead to a significant reduction in the amount of search that is needed to identify the referent. It has been argued that spatial information reduces the cognitive load (measured by eye tracking) necessary for resolving a referring expression (Paraboni et al., 2017). This research area (Krahmer and van Deemter, 2012; Ghanimifard and Dobnik, 2017) distinguishes between spatial referring expressions that involve another object in the description (e.g. "the rabbit in the hat") from those that do not (e.g. "the rabbit on the left"). The first group of expressions is known as *relational*, while we shall refer to the second one as *absolute*. A further distinction is made between referring expressions that are singular (e.g. "the rabbit in the hat") and those that are plural (e.g. "the three rabbits on the table") and refer to a *group* (see e.g., Lønning (1997); Gatt and van Deemter (2007); Krahmer and van Deemter (2012)).

In this paper, we classify GuessWhat?! spatial questions using *absolute*, *relational* and *group* distinctions and examine how LXMERT performs for each type of spatial question. We also conduct an error analysis and an attention analysis taking these categories into consideration.

Recent work by Agarwal et al. (2020) shows that in current visual dialogue datasets the dialogue history rarely matters. The authors ask crowdsourcers whether they can confidently answer a question by looking at the image and the question, without seeing the dialogue history. In our qualitative analysis we check whether history plays a role for the spatial questions of the GuessWhat?! game that LXMERT fails to answer.

## 3 Models

In this section we present the models that we compare. We also explain how we adapted LXMERT to the Oracle task. The models are trained on successful games.

**LSTM** is the baseline model proposed in de Vries et al. (2017). It does not have access to the raw image features. It receives as input embeddings of the target object's category, its spatial coordinates, and one question encoded by a dedicated LSTM. These three embeddings are concatenated and fed to a Multi-Layer Perceptron (MLP) that gives an answer (Yes or No).

**V-LSTM** We enhance the LSTM model described above with the visual modality and we remove the information about the target object category. We extract the visual vectors corresponding to the input image and the crop of the target object using a frozen ResNet-152 network pre-trained on ImageNet (He et al., 2016) and we pass them through a linear layer and a *tanh* activation function. We concatenate these scaled representations to the embeddings of the target object's spatial coordinates and the question: the resulting vector is fed to an MLP to obtain the answer, as it happens in the LSTM model.

**LXMERT** To evaluate the performance of a universal multimodal encoder, we employ LXMERT (Learning Cross-Modality Encoder Representations from Transformers) (Tan and Bansal, 2019). It represents an image by the set of position aware object embeddings for the 36 most salient regions detected by Faster R-CNN and it processes the text input by position aware randomly initialized word embeddings. We fill the 36th position with the visual features of the target object. Both the visual and linguistic representations are processed by a specialized transformer encoder based on self-attention layers; their outputs are then processed by a cross-modality encoder that through a cross-attention mechanism generates representations of the single modality (language and visual output) enhanced with the other modality as well as their joint representation (cross-modality output). LXMERT uses the special tokens CLS and SEP; the latter is used to separate sequences and to denote the end of the textual input. LXMERT has been pre-trained on five tasks.[1] It has 19 attention layers: 9 and 5 self-attention layers in the language and visual encoders, respectively and 5 cross-attention layers. We process the output corresponding to the CLS token. We consider both the pre-trained version (**LXMERT**) and the one trained from scratch (**LXMERT-S**).[2]

[1]Masked cross-modality language modeling, masked object prediction via RoI-feature regression, masked object prediction via detected-label classification, cross-modality matching, and image question answering.

[2]We have also evaluated a simplified version of LXMERT-S in which we use 6 self (4 language and 2 visual) and 2 cross-modal attention layers. The model behaves similarly to the more complex version trained from scratch.

| | | Single label | Multi labels |
|---|---|---|---|
| | Entity | 39269 | 39269 |
| | Not classified | 7925 | 7925 |
| ATTRIBUTE | Spatial | 29845 | 39250 |
| | Color | 7145 | 15403 |
| | Action | 3063 | 7645 |
| | Size | 532 | 1364 |
| | Texture | 538 | 901 |
| | Shape | 166 | 301 |

Table 1: Question type distribution in successful games following the classification proposed in (Shekhar et al., 2019) where a question can be assigned to more than one attribute type (multiple labels); the Single label column reports the number of questions which have been assigned to only one type.

## 4 The Dataset

The GuessWhat?! dataset is composed of more than 150k human-human dialogues containing an average of 5.3 questions in natural language created by turkers playing the game on MS COCO images (Lin et al., 2014). Humans have succeeded on 85% of the games. Not successful games may contain errors made by the human oracle which lead to task failure, we discard questions that belong to human dialogues that were not successful. The remaining set contains around 672K questions which are grounded on about 63K unique images and belong to about 135K dialogues.

Shekhar et al. (2019) propose a classification of the questions based on their focus distinguishing questions which ask about the entity of the target ("Is it an animal?" or "Is it a dog?") or an attribute of it. A question can focus on just one attribute (e.g., "Is it the black dog"? or "Is it black?") in which case it is assigned just to one attribute question type (color in the examples) or about more attributes (e.g., "does it have orange pillows on it?") in which case it is assigned to more attribute question types (to both color and spatial information in the example.) Table 1 reports their distribution in the human-human dialogues giving the numbers of questions assigned to one or more types (multi label) or to just one type (single label).

We conjecture that the spatial question type includes questions posing different challenges to multimodal models. Krahmer and van Deemter (2012) divide spatial expressions into *relational* (e.g. "the rabbit in the hat"), that specifies the location of the referent of a noun phrase (the target, "rabbit") relative to another object (the landmark, "hat"), and *absolute* that focus only on the target by providing locative information about it (e.g. "the rabbit on the left"). A third spatial expression that has received attention within the REG community are group referring expressions whose target is a group of entities (e.g. "the three rabbits on the table") or some specific entity of a the group to which the expression refers by ordering them (e.g. "the second rabbit from the left").

We adapt such classification to the GuessWhat?! spatial questions and classify them into four types: relational, absolute, group and other. To distinguish these types we have leveraged syntactic and lexical characteristics specific to each. Relational questions usually include a prepositional phrase followed by a noun phrase that includes either a pronoun (e.g. "Is there a sink directly above it?") or an object word (e.g. "is it the pen behind the laptop?"). Absolute spatial questions (e.g. "the one on the left?") instead contain a location word either in the $x$ axis (e.g. right, middle, left), or the $y$ (top, bottom), or the $z$ (e.g. front, back) axis. We also consider absolute those questions that include a spatial adjective in its superlative form (e.g. "the leftmost one?"). Finally, we consider group questions those containing a number which may indicate order (e.g. "right to left, is it the first one?") or groups (e.g. "in the back among four women?"). We have automatically annotated spatial questions by identifying nouns, prepositions and number using the Part of Speech tagger Stanza (Qi et al., 2020). When a question is not assigned to any of the three groups, we include it in the "Other" category.[3] We tried identifying objects using the entity recognizers included in Stanford core NLP (Manning et al., 2014) and Stanza (Qi et al., 2020) but the coverage was not good.

In the next section, we will first compare models using the multi-label classification reported in Table 1, then we will zoom into the spatial questions which together with the entity questions constitute the large majority of questions asked by humans. In order to understand strength and limits of multimodal models in answering spatial questions, we focus on those which are assigned only to the spatial question type to avoid confounding effects. Table 2 reports number of such sub-set.

| | % | Example |
|---|---|---|
| Relational | 31.9 | Is it the pen behind the PC? |
| Absolute | 31.8 | Is it the one on the left? |
| Group | 17.3 | Is it among the 4 women? |
| Other | 19.0 | Can you sleep on it? |

Table 2: Sub-type spatial questions distribution in successful games of questions annotated with only the spatial label in the test set (total: 29845).

## 5 Experiments

### 5.1 Evaluation by Question Type

de Vries et al. (2017) shows that the "blind" version of the LSTM model performs better that the version receiving the visual features. This result is heavily dependent on the question type distribution in human-human dialogues. As we have seen, entity questions are a great proportion of the questions humans ask. The "blind" baseline model is facilitated in answering them, since it is given the category of the target object. Following Mazuecos et al. (2020), we evaluate models accuracy by question types. As we can see from Table 3, the higher overall accuracy reached by the "blind" LSTM model is indeed mostly due to the "entity" questions for which it reaches 94% (questions like: "is it a vehicle?"). As expected, when removing the category (V-LSTM) the accuracy on answering questions about entities decreases to a large degree, but the use of visual features helps the model to answer color questions better. The replacement of the LXMERT architecture, together with the use of positional aware embedding representations of the image, bring an important boost in the accuracy: LXMERT trained from scratch outperforms the LSTM based model on all types of questions. The pre-training phase further increases the performance in important ways.

### 5.2 Evaluation on Spatial Questions

Above we have seen that LXMERT outperforms the other models on the spatial questions. Our fine-grained classification sheds light on an interesting point: its main advantage comes from the *relational* questions (Table 4). *Absolute* questions require cross-modal attention only to align a word with its referent, whereas *relational* questions are

[3] Examples of questions following into the "Other" category are: "Is it the tree outside?" – i.e. an elliptical question which could be completed as "Is it the tree outside the fenced garden?" – or "Can you sleep on it?" which is not about a spatial property that occurs in the image but an afforded one.

| | LSTM | V-LSTM | LXMERT-S | LXMERT |
|---|---|---|---|---|
| Entity | 93.37 | 83.24 (-10.13) | 88.64 (-4.73) | 91.09 (-2.28) |
| Spatial | 67.30 | 66.40 (-0.90) | 71.31 (+4.01) | 77.00 (+9.70) |
| Color | 61.64 | 68.06 (+6.42) | 70.51 (+8.87) | 76.42 (+14.78) |
| Action | 64.32 | 65.44 (+1.12) | 70.23 (+5.91) | 77.16 (+12.84) |
| Size | 60.41 | 62.76 (+2.35) | 67.23 (+6.82) | 75.44 (+15.03) |
| Texture | 69.92 | 66.15 (-3.77) | 71.92 (+2.00) | 77.47 (+7.55) |
| Shape | 68.44 | 64.12 (-4.32) | 70.76 (+2.32) | 74.42 (+5.98) |
| Not classified | 75.02 | 70.45 (-4.57) | 74.94 (-0.08) | 82.18 (+7.16) |
| Total | 75.94 | 72.70 (-3.24) | 77.41 (+1.47) | 82.21 (+6.27) |

Table 3: Accuracy of the models on the successful games by question type based on the multi label assignment. Values in parenthesis report the comparison with LSTM.

| | Absolute | Relational | Group |
|---|---|---|---|
| LSTM | 76.4 | 67.1 | 63.3 |
| V-LSTM | 75.2 | 63.5 | 62.8 |
| LXMERT-S | 80.5 | 69.6 | 68.4 |
| LXMERT | 83.4 | 77.2 | 71.6 |

Table 4: Accuracy of the sub-type of spatial questions (successful games, questions assigned only one type)

more challenging: the model has to locate the regions corresponding to the two related words and understand the relation holding among them. The *group* questions may require "counting" skills that go beyond the scope of this paper.

## 6 Qualitative Analysis

As a first step towards a deeper understanding of LXMERT performance, we use a linear logistic regression model for the task of predicting whether a question was answered correctly. In Shekhar et al. (2018) it has been shown that unsuccessful games contain more objects in the image than successful ones, and that the target size area is smaller. We use these two features as predictor variables together with the length of the question and the turn in which it was asked in the full dialogue. We observe that the number of objects in the image and the question turn play a significant role in predicting the model behaviour. This might be due to the fact that models do not receive the dialogue history as input. Below we run an error analysis based on the three spatial sub-type questions described above to check whether indeed this could be a source of error. After the error analysis, we study whether LXMERT uses its cross-modal attention differently across these three groups of questions.

### 6.1 Error Analysis

We did a manual error analysis of 20% of LXMERT errors on spatial questions. We tagged emergent error categories by following a qualitative annotation methodology. Below we describe our findings by classifying them in the three types of spatial questions that we consider throughout the paper.

We found that absolute and group questions have more errors related to the missing dialogue history than relational questions even though we explicitly allow for relational questions that include anaphoric pronouns. For these two categories, around 50% of errors are related to missing dialogue history. Dialogue history dependency in the dataset is generally not lexicalized with explicit pronouns but left implicit through ellipsis (e.g. "in the middle?"). Figure 2 shows an example of this. Question 5 could be answered with "yes" if asked at the beginning of the dialogue ("middle" would refer to the middle of the image) but its answer is "no" due to history ("middle" refers to the middle of the group of oranges). In most of these dialogues, the category of the target is left implicit because it is established in previous questions (e.g., "orange"). But also other information is implicit. For example, "the last single one?" does not say that the search is evolving from right to left. In these cases, the meaning of the question is only correctly interpretable in the dialogue context.

History dependence, as illustrated in Figure 2, is hard to detect even for human annotators. Using the presence of the pronoun to detect whether a question needs the history in order to be properly answered, as it has been done in Agarwal et al. (2020), might be misleading. Our examples show that ellipses might create more context dependen-

| Human question | Human answer |
|---|---|
| 1. It is a fruit? | yes |
| 2. It is the orange? | yes |
| 3. One of them I suppose? | yes |
| 4. Is it to our right? | no |
| 5. In the middle? | no |
| 6. The last single one? | yes |

Figure 2: Sample image and dialogue from the GuessWhat?! dataset. The red boxes mark the objects involved in the questions, while the green box marks the actual referent. LXMERT incorrectly answers "yes" to question 5. LXMERT, like all Oracles, does not have access to the dialogue history. It probably interprets the question as "is the target in the middle of the picture?". The image and dialogue illustrates the history dependence of questions.

cies and that there are questions which could be apparently answered even when given in isolation but they would be answered differently based on the context they are in.

For absolute only questions, we found the following errors. Questions related to the z-axis of the picture (e.g. "is it in the background?") seem to be harder for the model than those questions related to the x-axis of the picture (e.g. "is it on the left?"). The errors that do occur on the x-axis are either related to the fact that the dialogue history is necessary in order to interpret the question as in Figure 2, or that the target is neither on the left nor on the right of the x-axis. In this dataset the adjective left and right behave as vague adjectives. Questions that include superlatives (e.g."the rightmost book?) cause many errors. As well as questions that combine two or more of these characteristics (e.g. "is it the animal at the very front on the left ?"). Finally, the ambiguity of the word "middle", which could be used for any axis, seems to confuse the model.

For group questions, the second most frequent errors corresponds to questions grouping in one of the three axes. The term "row" is often used to group the target with other objects, especially when images are overcrowded with objects belonging to the same category. However, the term is an ambiguous one, as it can refer to any of the three axes and its meaning is often dependent on which interpretation is more salient in the image. Furthermore, inverse x-axis properties (e.g., "third girl from right?") also seem to be problematic. Another frequent error type includes questions that require counting above three (e.g., "seventh bus from the left?"). People can immediately and precisely identify that an image contains 1, 2, 3 or 4 items by a simple glance, this ability is called subitizing (Kaufman et al., 1949; Piazza et al., 2002). Identifying

| Layer | Absolute | Relational | Group |
|---|---|---|---|
| 0 | 3.9 | 4.1 | 3.3 |
| 1 | 4.2 | 4.6 | 4.1 |
| 2 | 3.8 | 4.5 | 4.0 |
| 3 | 3.7 | 4.0 | 3.7 |
| 4 | 1.3 | 2.2 | 1.9 |

Table 5: Language to Vision attention in LXMERT: Number of regions of the image considered salient in the last layer from the CLS token – viz. regions with an attention value higher than the 0.05 threshold.

the quantity of a larger number of objects takes considerably longer and involves counting for humans. It seems models such as LXMERT are able to do subitizing, but not counting. Other problematic group questions are multi-type ones, for instance belonging also to the relational type (e.g., "are there two of them on the branch?"); and questions using entities outside the image as reference, such as the viewers (e.g., "is it in the first room closer to us?").

For relational questions we find that a source of errors is when the target and the landmark bounding boxes overlap or one is included in the other ("is it the clock behind the person?"). Also when the landmark is a part of another object instead of being an object with well delimited borders the model seems to get confused ("is it under his feet?"). Questions that include non projective prepositions seem harder ("is it the person near the bicycle?") than those whose prepositions indicate the direction of the relation. Another source of errors are questions in which the landmark is large and no clear borders are visible ("is it on the water?"). Finally, those questions that require OCR (optical character recognition) are problematic ("does it have words on it?").

is it the bus on the left? No    is it the boat next to a car? No    is it one of the two in the back? Yes

Figure 3: Attentions from the CLS: in absolute questions attention is mostly on the only object the question refers to (the left bus, 0.13) and the target object (0.64) (**left**); in the relational questions attentions spread between the two related objects (car and boat, 0.12 each) and the target object (the boat on the back, 0.9) (**middle**); in the group questions attentions goes to the entity of the referred group (0.08 and 0.13) and the target (0.37) (**right**).

### 6.2 LXMERT's Attention

Here we aim to understand how LXMERT uses attention mechanisms to answer spatial questions. We focus our analysis on the cross-attention layers from language to vision. Recall that, in our adaptation of LXMERT to the Oracle task, the crop of the target is given as the 36th visual embedding together with the most salient regions of the image detected by Faster R-CNN. We are interested in understanding how it exploits the target visual representation to guide attention.

The entropy of the attention maps shows that the model in the first attention layers distributes attention across all regions (its entropy is close to the maximum possible level), at layer 2 it learns to focus its attention on some regions of the image and on the crop of the target. Finally, at the last layer, the attention on the CLS (the embedding given to the classifier to select the answer) reveals an interesting difference among question types: the number of regions considered salient in the absolute questions is lower that the one of salient regions in the group and relational questions. Table 5 reports the numbers of regions with an attention value higher than 0.05.[4] We have used different thresholds to compute the number of top-valued regions and the same pattern emerges. From a manual inspection, we have seen that the higher number of salient regions in the relational questions often is due to the fact that they refer to more candidate objects, differently from the absolute ones which usually refer to fewer or even just one object.

Figure 3 illustrates how LXMERT uses its attention in three sub-type of spatial questions. As we can see, when it interprets relational questions involving two objects, it "looks" both at the target (the boat) and the landmark (the car); in the example it answers the question negatively since the target of the game is the boat marked by the green box and not the one to which the question refers to. Similarly, when interpreting a group question, it looks at the referred group (the two giraffes); in the example it answers the question positively since the target of the game is indeed within the referred group. By looking at the attention maps, we noticed that interesting patterns emerge when looking at the attentions from the CLS token (Figure 3 marks the regions considered more salient from the CLS token). Other tokens put attention mostly or only on the target object region.

## 7 Conclusion

In this paper we tackle the problem of grounding spatial questions in the GuessWhat?! visual dialogue game. We adapt LXMERT to play the role of the Oracle of the GuessWhat?! game reaching an overall accuracy of 82.21%. This result outperforms the widely used baseline model by 6.27%. The gain is even higher for spatial questions, where LXMERT outperforms the baseline by 9.70%. In order to perform an in-depth analysis, we classify spatial questions into three sub-types and use this classification to annotate the subset of spatial questions in the GuessWhat?! test set. The fine-grained evaluation shows that the hardest spatial questions are the relational and group ones. We perform an in-depth analysis of LXMERT cross-modal attention and an qualitative analysis of the errors on each question sub-type. First of all, we find out that LXMERT puts attention on more regions when processing relational questions compared to absolute and group questions. Secondly, the qualitative analysis highlights the importance of having access to the dialogue history in order to answer some spatial questions. We leave this for future work.

[4]If the attention is equally distributed among all the 36 regions, their attention value would be 0.02 (viz. 1/36).

## References

Shubham Agarwal, Trung Bui, Joon-Young Lee, Ioannis Konstas, and Verena Rieser. 2020. History for visual dialog: Do we really need it? In *Proceedings of the 58th Annual Meeting of the Association for Computational Linguistics*, pages 8182–8197, Online. Association for Computational Linguistics.

Jason Baldridge, Tania Bedrax-Weiss, Daphne Luong, Srini Narayanan, Bo Pang, Fernando Pereira, Radu Soricut, Michael Tseng, and Yuan Zhang. 2018. Points, paths, and playscapes: Large-scale spatial language understanding tasks set in the real world. In *Proceedings of the First International Workshop on Spatial Language Understanding*, New Orleans. Association for Computational Linguistics.

Guillem Collell and Marie-Francine Moens. 2018. Learning representations specialized in spatial knowledge: Leveraging language and vision. *Transactions of the Association for Computational Linguistics*, 6:133–144.

Abhishek Das, Satwik Kottur, Khushi Gupta, Avi Singh, Deshraj Yadav, José M.F. Moura, Devi Parikh, and Dhruv Batra. 2017. Visual Dialog. In *Proceedings of the IEEE Conference on Computer Vision and Pattern Recognition*, pages 326–335.

Zhe Gan, Yu Cheng, Ahmed El Kholy, Linjie Li, Jingjing Liu, and Jianfeng Gao. 2019. Multi-step reasoning via recurrent dual attention for visual dialog. In *Proceedings of the 57th Annual Meeting of the Association for Computational Linguistics*, pages 6463–6474.

Albert Gatt and Kees van Deemter. 2007. Incremental generation of plural descriptions: Similarity and partitioning. In *EMNLP-CoNLL 2007, Proceedings of the 2007 Joint Conference on Empirical Methods in Natural Language Processing and Computational Natural Language Learning, June 28-30, 2007, Prague, Czech Republic*, pages 102–111.

Mehdi Ghanimifard and Simon Dobnik. 2017. Learning to compose spatial relations with grounded neural language models. In *IWCS 2017 - 12th International Conference on Computational Semantics - Long papers*.

Janosch Haber, Tim Baumgärtner, Ece Takmaz, Lieke Gelderloos, Elia Bruni, and Raquel Fernández. 2019. The PhotoBook dataset: Building common ground through visually-grounded dialogue. In *Proceedings of the 57th Annual Meeting of the Association for Computational Linguistics*.

Kaiming He, Xiangyu Zhang, Shaoqing Ren, and Jian Sun. 2016. Deep residual learning for image recognition. In *Proceedings of the IEEE conference on computer vision and pattern recognition*, pages 770–778.

Nikolai Ilinykh, Sina Zarrieß, and David Schlangen. 2019. Tell Me More: A Dataset of Visual Scene Description Sequences. In *Proceedings of the 12th International Conference on Natural Language Generation*.

Justin Johnson, Bharath Hariharan, Laurens van der Maaten, Li Fei-Fei, C. Lawrence Zitnick, and Ross B. Girshick. 2017. CLEVR: A diagnostic dataset for compositional language and elementary visual reasoning. In *IEEE Conference on Computer Vision and Pattern Recognition*, volume abs/1612.06890.

Kushal Kafle and Christopher Kanan. 2017. An analysis of visual question answering algorithms. In *Proceedings of the IEEE International Conference on Computer Vision*, pages 1965–1973.

E. L. Kaufman, M. Lord, T. Reese, and J. Volkmann. 1949. The discrimination of visual number. *The American journal of psychology*, page 498–525.

John D. Kelleher and Simon Dobnik. 2017. What is not where: the challenge of integrating spatial representations into deep learning architectures. In *In CLASP Papers in Computational Linguistics. Proceedings of the Conference on Logic and Machine Learning in Natural Language*, pages 41–52.

Emiel Krahmer and Kees van Deemter. 2012. Computational generation of referring expressions: A survey. *Computational Linguistics*, 38(1):173–218.

Tsung-Yi Lin, Michael Maire, Serge Belongie, James Hays, Pietro Perona, Deva Ramanan, Piotr Dollár, and C. Lawrence Zitnick. 2014. Microsoft COCO: Common objects in context. In *Computer Vision - ECCV 2014 - 13th European Conference, Zurich, Switzerland, September 6-12, 2014, Proceedings, Part V*, pages 740–755. Springer.

J. Lønning. 1997. Plurals and collectivity. In J. van Benthem and A. ter Meulen, editors, *Handbook of Logic and Language*, pages 1009–1054. Elsevier.

Christopher D. Manning, Mihai Surdeanu, John Bauer, Jenny Finkel, Steven J. Bethard, and David McClosky. 2014. The Stanford CoreNLP natural language processing toolkit. In *Association for Computational Linguistics (ACL) System Demonstrations*, pages 55–60.

Mauricio Mazuecos, Alberto Testoni, Raffaella Bernardi, and Luciana Benotti. 2020. On the role of effective and referring questions in GuessWhat?! In *Proceedings of the First Workshop on Advances in Language and Vision Research*, pages 19–25, Online. Association for Computational Linguistics.

Vishvak Murahari, Prithvijit Chattopadhyay, Dhruv Batra, Devi Parikh, and Abhishek Das. 2019. Improving generative visual dialog by answering diverse questions. In *Proceedings of the 2019 Conference on Empirical Methods in Natural Language Processing and the 9th International Joint Conference on Natural Language Processing*, pages 1449–1454.

Wei Pang and Xiaojie Wang. 2020. Visual dialogue state tracking for question generation. In *Proceedings of 34th AAAI Conference on Artificial Intelligence*.

Ivandré Paraboni, Kees van Deemter, and Judith Masthoff. 2007. Generating referring expressions: Making referents easy to identify. *Computational Linguistics*, 33(2):229–254.

Ivandré Paraboni, Alex Gwo Jen Lan, Matheus Mendes de Sant'Ana, and Flávio Luiz Coutinho. 2017. Effects of cognitive effort on the resolution of overspecified descriptions. *Computational Linguistics*, 43(2):451–459.

M. Piazza, A. Mechelli, B. Butterworth, and C.J. Price. 2002. Are subitizing and counting implemented as separate or functionally overlapping processes? *NeuroImage*, pages 435–446.

Peng Qi, Yuhao Zhang, Yuhui Zhang, Jason Bolton, and Christopher D. Manning. 2020. Stanza: A python natural language processing toolkit for many human languages. In *Proceedings of the 58th Annual Meeting of the Association for Computational Linguistics: System Demonstrations*, pages 101–108, Online. Association for Computational Linguistics.

Lee Sang-Woo, Gao Tong, Yang Sohee, Yao Jaejun, and Ha Jung-Woo. 2019. Large-scale answerer in questioner's mind for visual dialog question generation. In *Proceedings of International Conference on Learning Representations, ICLR*.

Ravi Shekhar, Tim Baumgärtner, Aashish Venkatesh, Elia Bruni, Raffaella Bernardi, and Raquel Fernandez. 2018. Ask no more: Deciding when to guess in referential visual dialogue. In *Proceedings of the 27th International Conference on Computational Linguistics*, pages 1218–1233, Santa Fe, New Mexico, USA. Association for Computational Linguistics.

Ravi Shekhar, Sandro Pezzelle, Yauhen Klimovich, Aurélie Herbelot, Moin Nabi, Enver Sangineto, and Raffaella Bernardi. 2017. FOIL it! Find one mismatch between image and language caption. In *Proceedings of the 55th Annual Meeting of the Association for Computational Linguistics (Volume 1: Long Papers)*, pages 255–265.

Ravi Shekhar, Aashish Venkatesh, Tim Baumgärtner, Elia Bruni, Barbara Plank, Raffaella Bernardi, and Raquel Fernández. 2019. Beyond task success: A closer look at jointly learning to see, ask, and GuessWhat. In *Proceedings of the 2019 Conference of the North American Chapter of the Association for Computational Linguistics: Human Language Technologies, Volume 1 (Long and Short Papers)*, pages 2578–2587.

Alane Suhr, Mike Lewis, James Yeh, and Yoav Artzi. 2017. A corpus of natural language for visual reasoning. In *Proceedings of the Annual Meeting of the Association for Computational Linguistics*, pages 217–223, Vancouver, Canada. Association for Computational Linguistics.

Hao Tan and Mohit Bansal. 2019. LXMERT: Learning cross-modality encoder representations from transformers. In *Proceedings of the 2019 Conference on Empirical Methods in Natural Language Processing and the 9th International Joint Conference on Natural Language Processing (EMNLP-IJCNLP)*, pages 5103–5114.

Alberto Testoni, Ravi Shekhar, Raquel Fernández, and Raffaella Bernardi. 2019. The devil is in the detail: A magnifying glass for the GuessWhich visual dialogue game. In *Proceedings of the 23rd SemDial Workshop on the Semantics and Pragmatics of Dialogue (LondonLogue)*, pages 15–24.

Harm de Vries, Florian Strub, Sarath Chandar, Olivier Pietquin, Hugo Larochelle, and Aaron C. Courville. 2017. Guesswhat?! visual object discovery through multi-modal dialogue. In *2017 IEEE Conference on Computer Vision and Pattern Recognition, CVPR 2017, Honolulu, HI, USA, July 21-26, 2017*, pages 4466–4475. IEEE Computer Society.

Terry Winograd. 1972. Understanding natural language. *Cognitive Psychology*, 3:1–191.

Tianhao Yang, Zheng-Jun Zha, and Hanwang Zhang. 2019. Making history matter: History-advantage sequence training for visual dialog. In *Proceedings of the International Conference on Computer Vision (ICCV)*.

Jiaping Zhang, Tiancheng Zhao, and Zhou Yu. 2018a. Multimodal hierarchical reinforcement learning policy for task-oriented visual dialog. In *Proceedings of the 19th Annual SIGdial Meeting on Discourse and Dialogue*, pages 140–150.

Junjie Zhang, Qi Wu, Chunhua Shen, Jian Zhang, Jianfeng Lu, and Anton van den Hengel. 2018b. Goal-oriented visual question generation via intermediate rewards. In *Proceedings of the European Conference of Computer Vision (ECCV)*, pages 186–201.

Rui Zhao and Volker Tresp. 2018. Improving goal-oriented visual dialog agents via advanced recurrent nets with tempered policy gradient. In *Proceedings of IJCAI*.

# Categorisation, Typicality & Object-Specific Features in Spatial Referring Expressions

**Adam Richard-Bollans**
University of Leeds, UK
mm15alrb@leeds.ac.uk

**Lucía Gómez Álvarez**
TU Dresden, Germany
lucia.gomez_alvarez@tu-dresden.de

**Anthony G. Cohn**
University of Leeds, UK
a.g.cohn@leeds.ac.uk

## Abstract

Various accounts of cognition and semantic representations have highlighted that, for some concepts, different factors may influence category and typicality judgements. In particular, some features may be more salient in categorisation tasks while other features are more salient when assessing typicality. In this paper we explore the extent to which this is the case for English spatial prepositions and discuss the implications for pragmatic strategies and semantic models. We hypothesise that object-specific features — related to object properties and affordances — are more salient in categorisation, while geometric and physical relationships between objects are more salient in typicality judgements. In order to test this hypothesis we conducted a study using virtual environments to collect both category and typicality judgements in 3D scenes. Based on the collected data we cannot verify the hypothesis and conclude that object-specific features appear to be salient in both category and typicality judgements, further evidencing the need to include these types of features in semantic models.

## 1 Introduction

Various accounts of cognition and semantic representations have highlighted that, for some concepts, different factors may influence category and typicality judgements (Smith et al., 1974; Rips, 1989). In particular, some features may be more salient in categorisation tasks while other features are more salient when assessing typicality. In this paper we explore the extent to which this is the case for English spatial prepositions and discuss the implications for pragmatic strategies and semantic models. We hypothesise that object-specific features — related to object properties and affordances — are more salient in categorisation, while geometric and physical relationships between objects are more salient in typicality judgements. In order to test this hypothesis we conducted a study using virtual environments to collect both category and typicality judgements in 3D scenes. Based on the collected data we cannot verify the hypothesis and conclude that object-specific features appear to be salient in both category and typicality judgements, further evidencing the need to include these types of features in semantic models.

The spatial prepositions we analyse are those considered to have a functional component as well as those prepositions that seem to act as their geometric counterpart. For the 'functional' prepositions, object affordances and functional relationships, such as *support* and *location control*, appear to be salient (Garrod et al., 1999; Coventry et al., 2001) compared to the geometric counterparts where geometric features and relative positions of objects appear to be more salient. In English, we consider the functional prepositions to be: 'in', 'on', 'over' and 'under'; and their respective geometric counterparts to be: 'inside', 'on top of', 'above' and 'below'. We also consider 'against' to be a functional preposition (Talmy, 1988), without a clear geometric counterpart.

To clarify the distinction between category and typicality judgements, we suppose that a category decision is when an entity is labelled with a category or concept and, though priming and context may certainly be factors, the judgement is not made in direct comparison with another entity. For example, a categorisation judgement occurs when an agent is asked whether 'the apple is *in* the bowl'. In order to reply, the agent judges the membership of the instance in the relevant category and the wider context plays a relatively minor role.

Typicality usually refers to the extent to which an entity is a good example of a concept — how similar it is to some ideal conceptual representation. In our study we ground the notion of typicality in comparison and preference — an entity, $x$, is more typical of a category than entity $y$ if, when



*Proceedings of the Third International Workshop on Spatial Language Understanding (SpLU 2020)*, pages 39–49
November 19, 2020. 
https://doi.org/10.18653/v1/P17

$x$ is compared with $y$, people in general pick $x$ as a better category member. For example, when requested to pick 'the apple *in* the bowl', an agent must compare a set of candidate objects for how well they fit the description.

By assessing typicality in this way we distinguish the notion of typicality from graded category membership. The typicality data that we collect does not arise from graded membership judgements where study participants are asked to assign a value of how well the concept fits the category, e.g. in (McCloskey and Glucksberg, 1978; Hampton, 1997), but instead from tasks in which participants select the best fitting instance from a given description.

In existing models of spatial language (and semantic models more generally), it is generally assumed that the underlying semantics of categorisation and typicality are essentially the same. However, as we will discuss in Section 4, appropriately distinguishing categorisation and typicality judgements is important when generating and processing referring expressions.

## 2 Background

Following various criticisms of definitional representations of concepts in human cognition (Wittgenstein, 1953), Rosch's Prototype Theory (Rosch, 1978) provided an approach based on family resemblance which does not presuppose that concepts have necessary and sufficient conditions for making category judgements. By relying on a degree of resemblance to some prototypical notion of a concept, category membership in this account may be treated as a matter of degree. With such an account it becomes appealing to conflate the notions of categorisation and typicality — the more an entity resembles a prototype the more likely it is to be labelled with the category *and* the more typical it is. There are however various accounts of concept analysis which suggest that category and typicality judgements are fundamentally different.

Smith et al. (1974) consider the influences of category decisions and propose a model to account for experimental findings. Central to the model is the 'characteristic feature assumption', which supposes that features vary in the extent to which they define a concept. Smith et al. suppose that there is a distinction in types of features — 'defining' features which strongly influence category judgements and 'characteristic' features which strongly influence typicality judgements — and give the example of 'robin' to illustrate this. For the concept 'robin', 'have wings' is an important defining feature relating to the categorisation of an entity as 'a robin', while 'perches in trees' is a characteristic feature which relates to how typical an entity is of 'a robin'.

Rips (1989) argued that categorisation of some entity is more than simply a judgement of how similar the entity is to some typical representation of the category. Rips provides support for this in an experiment where participants are asked to imagine an object of a given size and are asked which of two concepts, $A, B$ say, the object is more similar to and which the object is most likely to be. For the given concept pairs, e.g. 'pizza' and 'quarter', the hypothetical object may be considered more similar to one of the concepts yet more likely to be the other. In the case of the pizza and quarter, a round object with a three inch diameter is regarded as more similar to a quarter as pizzas are rarely so small, but more likely to be a pizza as the size of a quarter is generally fixed and is less than 3 inches.

This issue is explored further in (Osherson and Smith, 1997) where it is again argued that concept membership and typicality are distinct phenomena. Based on a study in (Berlin and Kay, 1991), Osherson and Smith argue that the notions differ using the seemingly extreme example of the concept 'red', even though it may be hard to imagine distinct defining and characteristic features for a concept with such simple semantics. However, the noted difference in judgements arises as people recognise particular wavelengths of light as being unambiguously red yet less typical than prototypical red. This difference in judgements preserves a monotonic relationship between category and typicality judgements i.e. if an entity, $x$, is a better category instance than $y$, then it is not less typical than $y$.

We believe that such monontonicity results offer a trivial case which may be explained without any fundamental modification of the underlying semantics or how they are processed. In the simple case of the colour red, we may represent the semantics in both categorisation and typicality judgements by considering the *dominant wavelength* — an instance is more or less typical and a better or worse category instance based on the similarity of the dominant wavelength to prototypical red and the distinction in category and typicality judgements is explained via a threshold which is applied in category judgements.

However, in the case of spatial language, the semantics are more complex and are influenced by a variety of geometric, functional and object-specific features. We believe that as a result, the relationship between typicality and categorisation may in fact be non-monotonic — there may be instances of a spatial preposition, $i_1, i_2$, such that $i_1$ is a better category member but less typical than $i_2$.

### 2.1 A note on terminology

Regarding the names of the objects being discussed we use *figure* (also known as: target, trajector, referent) to denote the entity whose location is important e.g. 'the **bike** next to the house' and *ground* (also known as: reference, landmark, relatum) to denote the entity used as a reference point in order to locate the figure e.g. 'the bike next to the **house**'. We call potential figure-ground pairs *configurations*.

### 2.2 Object-Specific Features

It is apparent that various object properties and affordances influence the categorisation and usage of spatial prepositions (Coventry et al., 1994; Feist and Gentner, 1998). For example, the animacy of the figure object may influence a decision to use 'in' or 'on'[1] (Feist and Gentner, 1998). Following (Coventry et al., 1994), we call these features 'object-specific' features.

We believe that these types of features provide a source of disagreement between category and typicality judgements and below for each of the functional prepositions we describe the object-specific features that are explored in this paper.

**In** As 'in' expresses a notion of *containment*, the ability of the ground to contain the figure is often salient whether or not the ground does in fact contain the figure in a geometric sense. Therefore, whether the ground is a type of container appears to be salient for 'in' (Coventry et al., 1994; Feist and Gentner, 1998; Richard-Bollans et al., 2019) and this may be considered a salient object-specific feature.

**Over/Under** 'over' and 'under' appear to have a 'covering' sense which is closely related to the functions of the figure and ground (Coventry et al., 2001; Tyler and Evans, 2001; Mori, 2019). For example, a covering object like a lid may exhibit this sense of 'over' when covering a container. Therefore, whether or not the figure is a covering object or the ground is a type of container may be salient object-specific features.

There is also a non-covering sense where a specific functional interaction exists between part of the figure and ground. For example, a tap may be 'over' a sink if only the spout of the tap is above the sink. Similarly, an object may be 'under' a lamp when the object is not under the lamp in a geometric sense but the light from the lamp shines on the object. These specific functional interactions rely on particular properties of the figure or ground and so we consider them to be object-specific features.

Relating to the functional interactions of the figure and ground, an intermediary object between the figure and ground may serve to block any functional interaction, as studied in (Coventry et al., 1994), and diminish the effect of any object-specific features which are present.

**Against** 'against' is commonly used to denote contact between two objects and as argued in (Herskovits, 1987) is more applicable in situations where the ground object is fixed and the figure is mobile. For example, one may describe a chair as being 'against a wall' but it would be odd to describe a wall as being 'against a chair'.

**On** 'on' is ubiquitous in the English language and is applied to many situations where usually at least one of the following hold: the figure is supported by the ground, the figure is above the ground or the figure is in contact with the ground. As a result, it is not clear that there are particular properties of figure or ground objects at table-top scales which create strong preferences for 'on'.

As discussed above, the preposition 'in' is often preferred when the ground object is a container. 'on' is therefore used less frequently in these scenarios (Feist and Gentner, 1998), even though the physical relationships between the objects often fulfil the requirements for 'on'. As a result, whether or not the ground is a container appears to be a salient object-specific feature for 'on'.

Finally, 'on' may be used to denote attachment of the figure to the ground. It is therefore plausible that, similarly to 'against', 'on' is more applicable in situations where the ground object is fixed relative to the figure.

[1] People were found to prefer 'in' when describing an inanimate figure (a coin) and 'on' when describing an animate figure (a firefly).

## 3 Hypothesis

Our main hypothesis is that categorisation and typicality judgements may differ for spatial prepositions in the following manner: given configurations $c_1, c_2$ and preposition $P$, participants may be more likely to categorise $c_1$ with $P$ yet more likely to select $c_2$ as a better instance of $P$. We hypothesise that this may arise in part because particular features are salient in category judgements which become less salient in typicality judgements. Note that under this hypothesis the relationship between categorisation and typicality is non-monotonic, making this in a sense stronger than the findings related to 'red' discussed by (Osherson and Smith, 1997).

In general, we expect that object-specific features will be more salient in categorisation while geometric and physical relationships, such as *containment* or *support*, will be more salient in typicality judgements.

Furthermore, we believe that this particular distinction may be more pronounced for the functional prepositions than for their geometric counterparts. This would be somewhat a corollary of the assumption that functionality in general is more salient for the former, for which tentative evidence is provided in (Richard-Bollans et al., 2020a) for these prepositions and (Coventry et al., 2001) in the case of 'over/above' and 'under/below'.

## 4 Generating & Understanding Referring Expressions

In this section we discuss the motivation for this investigation and the possible implications of a significant distinction between category and typicality judgements. In particular, we consider the ramifications for the field of Referring Expression Generation and Comprehension (REG/C), where noun phrases are used to identify entities e.g. 'the box under the table'.

Humans often prefer brief ambiguous descriptions over lengthy unambiguous descriptions (Rohde et al., 2012), and expressions involving spatial prepositions often fulfil this desire for brevity. For example, rather than referring to objects based on elaborate visual attributes like 'the yellow cup with two pink dots on it', humans often refer to objects using simple locative expressions, say 'the cup next to the stapler'. We also see many examples of expressions containing spatial prepositions in the SemEval-2014 corpus (Dukes, 2014) and the HuRIC corpus (Bastianelli et al., 2014), both of which consider natural language commands given to robots.

To explain why a distinction in category and typicality judgements is important in these scenarios, suppose we have a speaker and listener, intended referent, $r$, set of distractor objects[2] and suppose that the speaker is generating a description, $D$.

When the speaker generates an utterance in order to refer to $r$, there are various semantic and pragmatic considerations they must make. A naive model of such a speaker may simply find a concept within its vocabulary which is most suitable for $r$. This would clearly be a flawed strategy, however, as there may be other entities in the scene which better fit the concept — an expression may be true but not satisfy the speaker's communicative goals and so pragmatics must be considered. A more refined speaker model may find a description which best distinguishes $r$ from the distractor objects in $O$, similar to the algorithm of (Dale, 1989) which aims to maximise the *discriminatory power* of a description while minimising superfluous information.

It appears that the speaker must model how well an object fits a description compared to other objects (typicality judgement) and how well a description fits an object (category judgement). Further, it is apparent that humans will reason recursively about possible intentions of speakers and possible interpretations of listeners (Goodman and Frank, 2016), making these judgements also necessary for listeners.

Let us consider a more concrete example. Suppose we have a scenario as in Figure 1 where a bowl, $b$, is on a table and there is one cube, $c_{\text{red}}$, in it and one cube, $c_{\text{blue}}$, next to and not touching it. It seems plausible that humans are more likely to categorise the configuration ($c_{\text{blue}}$, $b$) with the preposition 'near' than the configuration ($c_{\text{red}}$, $b$) even though when comparing the configurations humans may agree that $c_{\text{red}}$ is more 'near' the bowl than $c_{\text{blue}}$.

Suppose a speaker gives an utterance 'the cube near the bowl' in order to refer to $c_{\text{blue}}$ which an agent must interpret. As may be expected, semantic models, e.g. (Platonov and Schubert, 2018), are likely to assign a better score for 'near' to ($c_{\text{red}}$, $b$) than ($c_{\text{blue}}$, $b$). If the system has a crude strategy

[2]A distractor object is an object in the scene which the speaker is not intending to refer to.

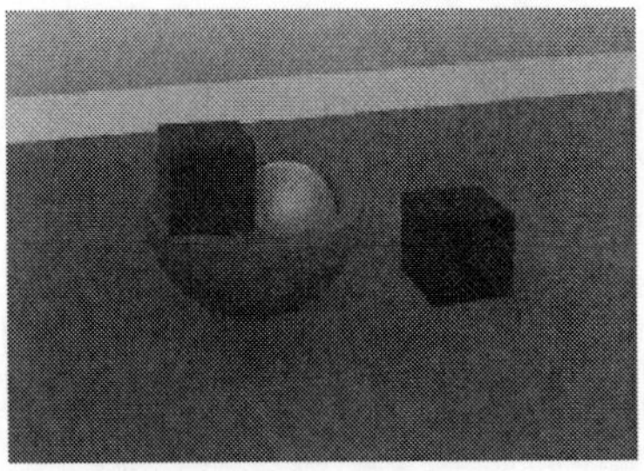

Figure 1: An example of possible confusion when not accounting for object-specific features.

for interpretation which simply selects the configuration with the highest semantic score, then such a system would erroneously select $c_{\text{red}}$.

Many systems with more sophisticated pragmatic strategies, e.g. (Golland et al., 2010), have been developed which aim to take into account and reason with the possible utterances available to the speaker. In this case, such a system may correctly select $c_{\text{blue}}$ if it recognises that other better utterances would have been available to the speaker if the intended referent was $c_{\text{red}}$. 'the cube in the bowl' would be a clear example of such an utterance which seems to clearly identify $c_{\text{red}}$ over $c_{\text{blue}}$. However, supposing that our hypothesis is correct, we contend that this marked distinction is not simply a matter of typicality and the fact that it would be unusual to categorise $(c_{\text{red}}, b)$ with 'near' is more salient than any distinction in typicality between the two configurations. As $c_{\text{red}}$ is not 'in' the bowl in an ideal sense we can imagine that a semantic model based simply on the physical relationships between the objects may provide a more marked distinction between the configurations for 'near' than for 'in'. In this case, 'the cube in the bowl' wouldn't necessarily seem like a better utterance to identify $c_{\text{red}}$ than 'the cube near the bowl'.

Moreover, even if typicality on its own works well for REC, understanding and modelling the differences between categorisation and typicality is important for producing *natural* utterances in REG. For instance, suppose the speaker creates an utterance where $r$ is more typical for the concept, $C$ say, in $D$ than any of the distractor objects. If categorisation is not aligned with typicality, such a strategy may produce unusual utterances where, though $r$ is typical for $C$, it is uncommon to categorise $r$ with $C$. Such unnatural utterances may trigger unwanted conversational implicatures and be a source of confusion. For example, the utterance 'the ball on the bowl' in the context of Figure 1 would be an unusual way to describe the ball as the preposition 'in' is often used with objects such as bowls. From this unconventional usage of 'on' a listener may imply that for some reason 'in' was not suitable e.g. if the speaker is actually referring to another unseen ball. The issue of producing natural utterances has been recognised by others in the field (Krishnaswamy and Pustejovsky, 2019) and is an important challenge to overcome if we are to develop more sophisticated REG systems.

With regards to existing models of spatial language, it is generally assumed that the underlying semantics of categorisation and typicality are essentially the same. For example, in the PRAGR mechanism proposed in (Mast et al., 2016) a pragmatic strategy is presented which aims to maximise both the *acceptability* and *discriminatory power* of a description. Acceptability is calculated using similarity to a prototype based on physical relationships while the discriminatory power is calculated considering the acceptability of the description for the referent compared to other distractor objects.

## 5 Data Collection

In order to investigate typicality measures and categorisation judgements in detail, we conducted a study which is described below. Collected data, details of the framework and results of the analysis can be found in the Leeds research data repository.[3] The latest version of the data collection environment and code for analysis can be found in the GitHub repository.[4]

### 5.1 Environment & Tasks

The data collection framework is built on the Unity3D[5] game development software, which provides ample functionality for the kind of tasks we implement. Two tasks were created for our study — a Categorisation Task and a Typicality Task. The former allows for the collection of categorical data while the latter provides typicality judgements.

In the Categorisation Task participants are shown a figure-ground pair (highlighted and with text description, see Figure 2) and asked to select *all* prepositions in the list which fit the configuration. Participants may select 'None of the above' if they deem none of the prepositions to be appropriate.

[3] https://doi.org/10.5518/873

[4] https://github.com/alrichardbollans/spatial-preposition-annotation-tool-unity3d

[5] https://unity.com/

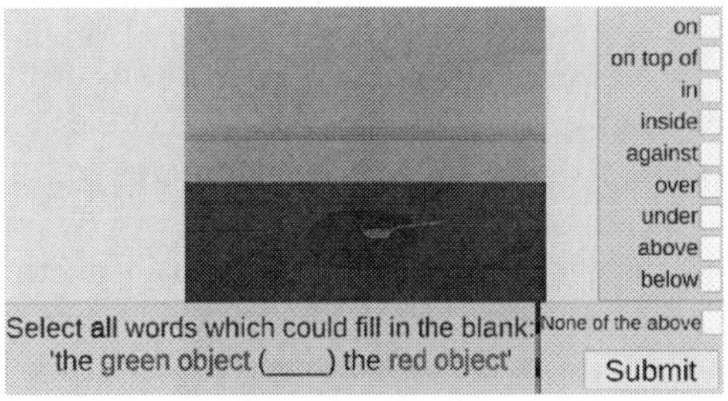


Figure 2: Categorisation Task

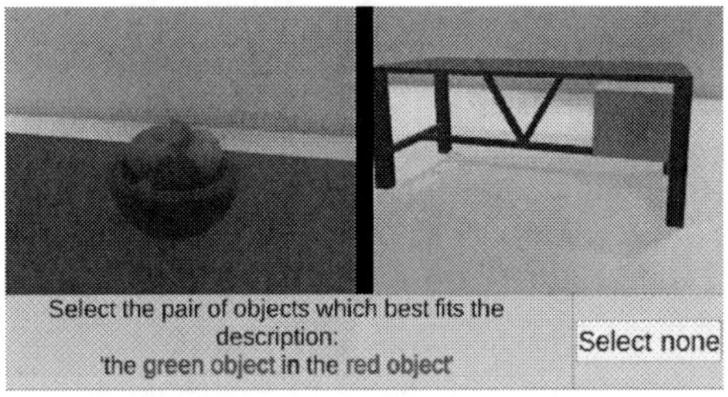


Figure 3: Typicality Task

Often categories and concepts are viewed as antagonistic entities; for example work on Conceptual Spaces is often concerned with comparison of categories, e.g. partitioning a feature space (Douven et al., 2013). We believe however that the vagueness present in spatial language is so severe that it is not clear that a meaningful model distinguishing the categories is possible. For this reason, participants in our studies are asked to select *all* possible prepositions for a configuration rather than a single best-fitting preposition.

In the Typicality Task participants are given a description and shown two configurations, see Figure 3. Participants are asked to select the configuration which *best fits* the description. Again, participants can select none if they deem none of the configurations to be appropriate.

In order to minimise differences in the tasks that may elicit different conceptualisations of objects in the scenes, the phrasing of the descriptions is the same in both the Categorisation Task and Typicality Task e.g. both tasks use the definite determiner 'the' and objects are referred to by their colour.

### 5.2 Scenes

We hypothesise that object-specific features strongly influence category decisions while the geometric ideals associated to the prepositions are more salient in typicality decisions. Scenes are therefore created for each preposition which vary the degree to which these object-specific features are present and also vary how similar the relational aspects of the configurations are to the geometric ideals associated with the given preposition. For example for the preposition 'in', we have a scene where the ground is a container and the figure is not very well contained in it and a scene where the ground is not a type of container but the figure is well contained in it. In this case, if the hypothesis is correct, we would expect a preference for categorisation in the former and a preference for typicality in the latter.

We have created 18 virtual 3D scenes each containing a single highlighted figure-ground pair. Four scenes each were created for 'in', 'on', 'over' and 'under' and these scenes were also shared with their respective geometric counterparts: 'inside', 'on top of', 'above' & 'below'. Two scenes were created for 'against'. In the Typicality Task, participants compare scenes/configurations associated with the preposition given in the description.

### 5.3 Study

The study was conducted online and participants from the university were recruited via internal mailing lists along with recruitment of friends and family.[6] Each participant performed first the Categorisation Task on 6 randomly selected scenes and then the Typicality Task on 15 randomly selected scenes, which took participants roughly 5 minutes. 30 native English speakers participated providing 180 annotations in the Categorisation Task and 447 annotations in the Typicality Task.

As the study was hosted online, we first asked participants to show basic competence. This was assessed by showing participants two simple scenes with an unambiguous description of an object. Participants are asked to select the object which best fits the description. If the participant makes an incorrect guess in either scene they are taken back to the start menu.

## 6 Results

In this section we use the collected data to test the hypothesis and conclude that we cannot verify the hypothesis. We propose that this is because object-specific features are in fact salient in both category and typicality judgements and provide examples to support this.

[6]University of Leeds Ethics Approval Code: MEEC 19-030. Participants were recruited without incentive.

Figure 4: The bin under the table

Figure 5: The notepad under the lamp

### 6.1 Comparing Categorisation & Typicality

To analyse the collected data, we consider pairs of tested configurations for each preposition and evaluate the degree to which category and typicality judgements differ. For each pair, $(c_1, c_2)$, we first decide whether $c_1$ is a genuinely better category instance than $c_2$ or is more typical than $c_2$. To do this we simply use a hypothesis test with significance level 10% and null hypothesis that the given configurations are equally likely to be labelled with the preposition (in the category case) or equally likely to be selected (in the typicality case). In the category case the p-value is calculated using the one-tailed version of Fisher's exact test. In the typicality case the p-value is simply: $p = \sum_{k=C_{1,2}}^{N} \binom{N}{k} \times 0.5^N$, where $N$ is the number of times the pair is tested and $C_{1,2}$ is the number of times $c_1$ is selected over $c_2$. In 22 out of the 49 given pairs, one of the configurations is a significantly better category instance or is more typical than the other.

Considering the somewhat trivial case, similar to the case of 'red' discussed in Section 2, where two entities are both unambiguous cases of a concept but one of the entities is more typical than the other; there is one instance of this in our dataset. For the preposition 'under' the configurations shown in Figures 4 & 5 were both always labelled with the preposition, out of seven tests in the former and ten tests in the latter, but the (bin, table) configuration in Figure 4 is significantly more typical than the (notepad, lamp) configuration in Figure 5. As previously discussed, however, this is an unsurprising result.

Regarding the main hypothesis of this paper, there are no pairs of configurations in our dataset where one of the configurations is a significantly better category member and the other is significantly more typical. Moreover, in only nine pairs is there any possible disagreement where one of the configurations is more often labelled with the preposition and the other configuration is more often selected in the Typicality Task — in all but one of these cases neither configuration is a significantly better category member or is significantly more typical. We therefore cannot conclude that our hypothesis is correct and it appears that the notions of categorisation and typicality do not significantly vary due to object-specific features — these appear to be both defining and characteristic features.

Clearly we have only tested a small number of features and there are a vast array of salient features for each preposition for which the hypothesis may still be correct. However, our results suggest that object-specific features are salient in both categorisation and typicality judgements — in some cases the object-specific features appear to have a stronger influence than the physical relationships. Interestingly, there is some tentative evidence that this extends in general to the geometric counterparts and suggests that these prepositions are not purely spatial — supporting findings in (Dobnik and Ghanimifard, 2020).

### 6.2 Importance of Object-Specific Features

In the following we provide some examples from our dataset which highlight the importance of object-specific features.

**On** For the preposition 'on', the (mug, pencil) configuration in Figure 6 is both a significantly better category member and is significantly more typical than the (pear, bowl) configuration in Figure 7. Regarding the physical relationships, (pear, bowl) appears to be a better example of 'on' than (mug, pencil). If we consider the usual salient features for 'on':

- The pear is fully *supported* by the bowl, while the mug is leaning on both the pencil and the table

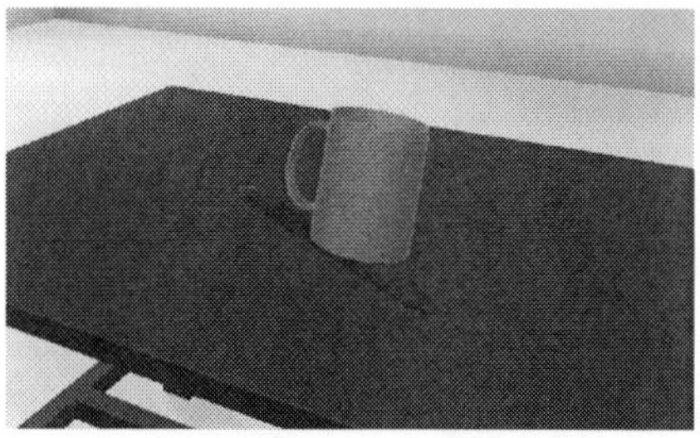

Figure 6: The mug on the pencil

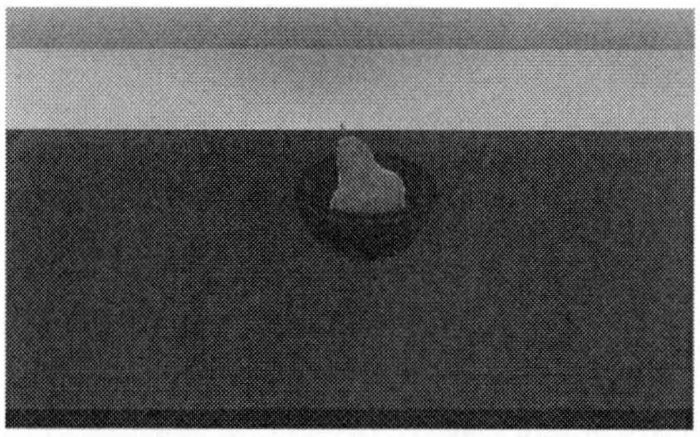

Figure 7: The pear in/on the bowl

- There is a high degree of *contact* between the pear and the bowl compared to the mug and pencil
- The entirety of the pear is *above* some part of the bowl, while the bottom of the mug is level with the bottom of the pencil

We therefore believe this result is not due to the physical relationships of (mug, pencil) better representing 'on' than (pear, bowl) and that this result arises primarily because 'on' is generally not used for containers. One may have expected this result if the objects in the experiments were named — 'on the bowl' sounds strange while 'on the pencil' seems more plausible. It is therefore even more surprising given that the objects were not named in a way that influences the decisions.

**In/Inside** For the prepositions 'in' and 'inside', the (pear, bowl) configuration in Figure 8 was more likely to be selected in the Typicality Task than the (cube, shelf) configuration in Figure 9. If we measure containment simply as the degree to which one object is contained in the bounding box or convex hull of another, as is common in grounded semantic models e.g. (Chang et al., 2014; Platonov and Schubert, 2018), then the cube would be fully contained by the shelf whereas the pear is not even partially contained by the bowl.

It therefore appears that the role of the bowl as a type of container is influencing typicality judgements for both these prepositions.

Figure 8: The pear in the bowl

Figure 9: The cube on/in the shelf

**Over/Above** For the preposition 'over', the (tap, sink) configuration in Figure 10 is both a significantly better category member and is significantly more typical than the (lid, pan) configuration in Figure 11. The same is true for the preposition 'above', though in this case the results are not significant.

Again, the physical relationships of (lid, pan) appear to better capture the geometric meanings of 'over' and 'above' than (tap, sink). There is also some functional interaction between the objects in both cases — lids are used to cover pans and sinks are placed below taps to catch the water. The preference for the (tap, sink) configuration is therefore

Figure 10: The tap over the sink

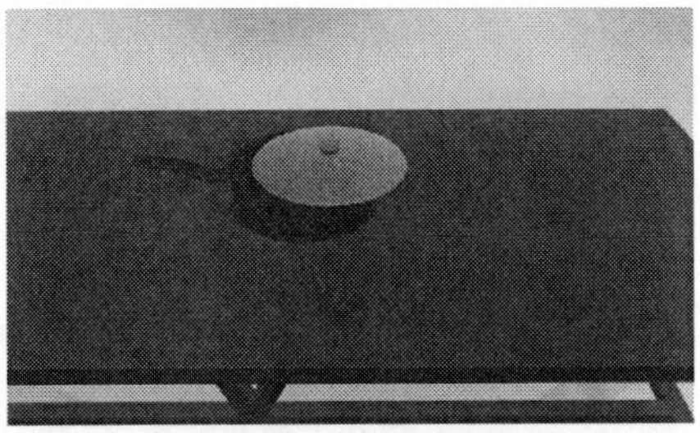

Figure 11: The lid over the pan

somewhat surprising.

However, the lid does not appear to be properly fulfilling its functional role, as it is not fully covering the container part of the pan. This may explain the preference for (tap, sink) and further highlight the importance of considering functional interactions based on usual object usages.

## 7 Discussion

Regardless of the hypothesis, these results highlight the importance of including object-specific features in semantic models of spatial language. With the possible exception of (Platonov and Schubert, 2018), these types of features are rarely included in semantic models and many systems are developed in block-world type environments, e.g. (Spranger, 2013; Mast et al., 2016; Perera et al., 2018), where these types of features are not needed.

One approach to improving semantic models may be to incorporate information from knowledge bases such as ConceptNet (Speer and Havasi, 2012) or AfNet (Varadarajan and Vincze, 2012). For example, from ConceptNet one can determine that lids are used for covering and that bowls are containers. Another approach is to leverage affordance detection systems, e.g. (Do et al., 2018), which use information from the scene to predict object affordances.

In (Rodrigues et al., 2020) some object-specific features, e.g. whether or not the ground is a type of container, are taken to distinguish separate polysemes.[7] By leveraging previous work on modelling the polysemy of spatial prepositions (Richard-Bollans et al., 2020b), it may be possible to incorporate object-specific features into a semantic model by using these features to distinguish polysemes. In order to carry this out, further work identifying salient object-specific features for each preposition would be beneficial and a larger dataset is needed which provides more instances of prepositions representing a greater variety of object-specific features.

[7] A word is said to exhibit *polysemy* where the word has multiple related senses. Each of these senses is called a *polyseme*.

## Acknowledgments

The first author is supported by an EPSRC Studentship; the final author is partially supported by an Alan Turing Institute Fellowship, and also by the EC AI4EU project under grant agreement 825619. We would also like to thank the reviewers for their constructive feedback.

## References

Emanuele Bastianelli, Giuseppe Castellucci, Danilo Croce, Luca Iocchi, Roberto Basili, and Daniele Nardi. 2014. HuRIC: a Human Robot Interaction Corpus. In *LREC*, pages 4519–4526.

Brent Berlin and Paul Kay. 1991. *Basic color terms: Their universality and evolution.* Univ of California Press.

Angel Chang, Manolis Savva, and Christopher D. Manning. 2014. Learning Spatial Knowledge for Text to 3D Scene Generation. In *Proc EMNLP*, pages 2028–2038. Association for Computational Linguistics.

Kenny R. Coventry, Richard Carmichael, and Simon C. Garrod. 1994. Spatial prepositions, object-specific function, and task requirements. *Journal of Semantics*, 11(4):289–309.

Kenny R. Coventry, Mercè Prat-Sala, and Lynn Richards. 2001. The Interplay between Geometry and Function in the Comprehension of Over, Under, Above, and Below. *Journal of Memory and Language*, 44(3):376–398.

Robert Dale. 1989. Cooking up referring expressions. In *Proceedings of 27th Annual Meeting of the association for Computational Linguistics*, pages 68–75. Association for Computational Linguistics.

Thanh-Toan Do, Anh Nguyen, and Ian Reid. 2018. AffordanceNet: An End-to-End Deep Learning Approach for Object Affordance Detection. In *Proceedings of 2018 IEEE international conference on robotics and automation*. IEEE.

Simon Dobnik and Mehdi Ghanimifard. 2020. Spatial Descriptions on a Functional-Geometric Spectrum: the Location of Objects. In *Proc German Conference on Spatial Cognition*, pages 219–234. Springer.

Igor Douven, Lieven Decock, Richard Dietz, and Paul Égré. 2013. Vagueness: A Conceptual Spaces Approach. *Journal of Philosophical Logic*, 42(1):137–160.

Kais Dukes. 2014. SemEval-2014 Task 6: Supervised Semantic Parsing of Robotic Spatial Commands. In *Proceedings of the 8th International Workshop on Semantic Evaluation*, pages 45–53.

Michele I Feist and Derdre Gentner. 1998. On plates, bowls, and dishes: Factors in the use of English IN and ON. In *Proc 20th annual meeting of the cognitive science society*, pages 345–349.

Simon Garrod, Gillian Ferrier, and Siobhan Campbell. 1999. In and on: investigating the functional geometry of spatial prepositions. *Cognition*, 72(2):167–189.

Dave Golland, Percy Liang, and Dan Klein. 2010. A Game-Theoretic Approach to Generating Spatial Descriptions. In *Proc EMNLP*, pages 410–419.

Noah D. Goodman and Michael C. Frank. 2016. Pragmatic language interpretation as probabilistic inference. *Trends in Cognitive Sciences*, 20(11):818–829.

James A. Hampton. 1997. Conceptual combination: Conjunction and negation of natural concepts. *Memory & Cognition*, 25(6):888–909.

Annette Herskovits. 1987. *Language and spatial cognition*. Cambridge University Press.

Nikhil Krishnaswamy and James Pustejovsky. 2019. Generating a Novel Dataset of Multimodal Referring Expressions. In *Proceedings of the 13th International Conference on Computational Semantics - Short Papers*, pages 44–51. Association for Computational Linguistics.

Vivien Mast, Zoe Falomir, and Diedrich Wolter. 2016. Probabilistic reference and grounding with PRAGR for dialogues with robots. *Journal of Experimental & Theoretical Artificial Intelligence*, 28(5):889–911.

Michael E. McCloskey and Sam Glucksberg. 1978. Natural categories: Well defined or fuzzy sets? *Memory & Cognition*, 6(4):462–472.

Souma Mori. 2019. A cognitive analysis of the preposition *over*: image-schema transformations and metaphorical extensions. *Canadian Journal of Linguistics*, 64(3):444–474.

Daniel Osherson and Edward E Smith. 1997. On typicality and vagueness. *Cognition*, 64(2):189–206.

Ian Perera, James Allen, Choh Man Teng, and Lucian Galescu. 2018. Building and Learning Structures in a Situated Blocks World Through Deep Language Understanding. In *Proc 1st International Workshop on Spatial Language Understanding*, pages 12–20.

Georgiy Platonov and Lenhart Schubert. 2018. Computational Models for Spatial Prepositions. In *Proc 1st International Workshop on Spatial Language Understanding*, pages 21–30.

Adam Richard-Bollans, Brandon Bennett, and Anthony G. Cohn. 2020a. Automatic generation of typicality measures for spatial language in grounded settings. In *Proceedings of 24th European Conference on Artificial Intelligence*.

Adam Richard-Bollans, Lucía Gómez Álvarez, Brandon Bennett, and Anthony G. Cohn. 2019. Investigating the dimensions of spatial language. In *Proceedings of Speaking of Location 2019: Communicating about Space*. CEUR Workshop Proceedings.

Adam Richard-Bollans, Lucía Gómez Álvarez, and Anthony G. Cohn. 2020b. Modelling the polysemy of spatial prepositions in referring expressions. In *Proceedings of 17th International Conference on Principles of Knowledge Representation and Reasoning*.

Lance J . Rips. 1989. Similarity, typicality, and categorization. In Stella Vosniadou and Andrew Ortony, editors, *Similarity and Analogical Reasoning*, 1st edition. Cambridge University Press.

Edilson J Rodrigues, Paulo E Santos, Marcos Lopes, Brandon Bennett, and Paul E Oppenheimer. 2020. Standpoint semantics for polysemy in spatial prepositions. *Journal of Logic and Computation*.

Hannah Rohde, Scott Seyfarth, Brady Clark, Gerhard Jäger, and Stefan Kaufmann. 2012. Communicating with cost-based implicature: A game-theoretic approach to ambiguity. In *Proceedings of 16th Workshop on the Semantics and Pragmatics of Dialogue*, pages 107–116.

Eleanor Rosch. 1978. Principles of categorization. In Eleanor Rosch and Barbara B. Lloyd, editors, *Cognition and Categorization*, volume 1, pages 27–78. Lawrence Erlbaum Associates, Hillsdale, NJ.

Edward E Smith, Edward J Shoben, and Lance J Rips. 1974. Structure and process in semantic memory: A featural model for semantic decisions. *Psychological review*, 81(3). Publisher: American Psychological Association.

Robert Speer and Catherine Havasi. 2012. Representing General Relational Knowledge in ConceptNet 5. In *LREC*, pages 3679–3686.

Michael Spranger. 2013. Grounded lexicon acquisition - case studies in spatial language. *2013 IEEE Third Joint International Conference on Development and Learning and Epigenetic Robotics (ICDL)*, pages 1–6.

Leonard Talmy. 1988. Force Dynamics in Language and Cognition. *Cognitive science*, 12(1):49–100.

Andrea Tyler and Vyvyan Evans. 2001. Reconsidering prepositional polysemy networks: the case of over. *Language*, 77(4):724–765.

Karthik Mahesh Varadarajan and Markus Vincze. 2012. Afnet: The affordance network. In *Asian Conference on Computer Vision*, pages 512–523. Springer.

Ludwig Wittgenstein. 1953. *Philosophical investigations*. Macmillan.

# A Hybrid Deep Learning Approach for Spatial Trigger Extraction from Radiology Reports

**Surabhi Datta, Kirk Roberts**
School of Biomedical Informatics
University of Texas Health Science Center at Houston
Houston TX, USA
{surabhi.datta, kirk.roberts}@uth.tmc.edu

## Abstract

Radiology reports contain important clinical information about patients which are often tied through spatial expressions. Spatial expressions (or triggers) are mainly used to describe the positioning of radiographic findings or medical devices with respect to some anatomical structures. As the expressions result from the mental visualization of the radiologist's interpretations, they are varied and complex. The focus of this work is to automatically identify the spatial expression terms from three different radiology sub-domains. We propose a hybrid deep learning-based NLP method that includes – 1) generating a set of candidate spatial triggers by exact match with the known trigger terms from the training data, 2) applying domain-specific constraints to filter the candidate triggers, and 3) utilizing a BERT-based classifier to predict whether a candidate trigger is a true spatial trigger or not. The results are promising, with an improvement of 24 points in the average F1 measure compared to a standard BERT-based sequence labeler.

## 1 Introduction

Radiology reports contain a radiologist's interpretations of an imaging study of a patient. The mental interpretations often get expressed through descriptions of important radiological entities with reference to a particular anatomical structure (Datta et al., 2020a). The radiological entities whose positions are described mainly include radiographic findings (e.g., clinical findings like *interstitial emphysema* and imaging observations like *ground-glass opacity*) and medical devices (e.g., *endotracheal tube* and *central venous catheter*). There exists a wide variation in the spatial language used by radiologists in expressing the exact positioning of the radiological entities. Limited research has focused on effectively identifying the spatial expressions from multiple imaging modalities. Therefore, the focus of this work is to investigate different automatic approaches to extract the spatial expressions from the report sentences along with highlighting the various challenges involved in this task. These extracted spatial expressions, if predicted accurately, can also facilitate clinical applications such as automatic labeling of radiographic images for training image classifiers (Wang et al., 2017).

Identification of spatial expressions in a sentence forms the foundation for other downstream spatial information extraction tasks. Much of the clinically relevant information appears in the context of a spatial expression. Consider the following sentence:

> *A lytic lesion* ***at*** *the left vertex* ***extending into*** *the epidural region, scalp and soft tissues is grossly unchanged in appearance.*

Here, we note that it is very crucial to accurately identify the spatial expressions such as *at* and *extending into*. Firstly, these trigger terms denote the specific positioning of the *lesion* by associating the *lesion* term with anatomical entities such as *left vertex* and *epidural region*. Secondly, this indirectly helps in identifying all the modifier information about the *lesion* including its density (i.e., *lytic*) and status (i.e., *unchanged in appearance*).

Spatial expressions are also used to describe the positioning of the medical devices that are inserted into specific body locations. Radiologists often document the current position status of the devices (e.g., *malpositioned, satisfactory position*) and often times indicate their changes in positioning. The following is an example of the radiologist's interpretation about a device position:

> *PICC line* ***enters from*** *left arm,* ***descends to*** *the lower inferior vena cava, then turns and* ***extends peripherally to*** *left subclavian vein.*



*Proceedings of the Third International Workshop on Spatial Language Understanding (SpLU 2020)*, pages 50–55
November 19, 2020. 
https://doi.org/10.18653/v1/P17

This captures the mental visualization of the radiologist as they interpret the specific position of the *PICC line* from the corresponding image. We note that there are diverse expressions belonging to multiple part-of-speech categories (e.g., verbs, prepositions, verbs followed by prepositions) that the radiologists use in documenting the spatial position of both findings and devices.

In this work, our aim is to identify all the spatial expressions given a radiology report sentence. We experiment with a pre-trained language model, BERT (Devlin et al., 2019), used as a sequence labeler to extract the spatial expressions (or triggers). We further propose a hybrid deep learning method where we use BERT as a classifier in combination with domain-dependent heuristics. Specifically, in this hybrid approach, we first extract the candidate trigger terms from the sentences with high recall leveraging the terms from the training corpus. We then filter the candidates by applying a set of radiology-specific constraints. Finally, we utilize BERT as a classification model to identify if each of the filtered candidate terms is a trigger expression or not.

## 2 Related Work

Some previous studies have focused on extracting spatial relations from radiology reports (Roberts et al., 2012; Rink et al., 2013). However, both these studies are specific to appendicitis-related reports. Our previous work has also aimed at identifying spatial expressions (mainly prepositional) from chest X-ray reports (Datta et al., 2020a; Datta and Roberts, 2020). Moreover, all these studies have focused on identifying spatial relations associated only with radiographic findings. We aim to identify more complex and varied spatial expressions associated with descriptions of both findings and medical devices. Importantly, descriptions of devices often utilize far richer spatial language, as shown in the *PICC line* example above.

Both in the general and medical domains, hybrid deep learning approaches have been used lately for various natural language processing (NLP) tasks such as document classification (Asim et al., 2019) and named entity recognition (Li et al., 2019). A recent work has also demonstrated the promising results of applying a hybrid approach for extracting clinical information from CT scan reports (Gupta et al., 2019). Moreover, many NLP tasks have leveraged the contextualized representations of pre-trained language models such as BERT. However, not much effort has been directed toward building hybrid methods based on BERT. Extracting spatial expressions from text often requires domain knowledge of language characteristics. Thus, we investigate the impact of combining radiology-specific constraints with a BERT-based model to extract spatial expressions from radiology reports.

| Item | Frequency |
|---|---|
| Spatial triggers | 1372 |
| POS sequence categories | 33 |

| Item | Frequency | Examples |
|---|---|---|
| Prepositions (IN) | 1093 | *within, throughout* |
| Verbs (VBG\|VBP\|VBZ\|VB\|VBD) | 163 | *demonstrate, shows* |
| Verb followed by preposition | 52 | *extending into, projected at* |
| Noun followed by preposition | 32 | *projects over, grows into* |
| Longest triggers (TO DT NN IN, PDT DT NN TO) | 7 | *to the left of, all the way to* |

Table 1: Corpus statistics of spatial expressions.

## 3 Dataset

We use a dataset of 400 radiology reports containing annotated spatial expressions (Datta et al., 2020b). These reports are taken from the MIMIC III clinical corpus (Johnson et al., 2016). Our dataset consists of an equal distribution of three different imaging modalities, namely, chest X-rays, brain MRIs, and babygrams. Some basic statistics related to the spatial expressions in this dataset are shown in Table 1. Note that this dataset includes multi-word spatial triggers and triggers with varied part-of-speech categories. This makes the task more challenging compared to using single word triggers, mostly prepositions as in Rad-SpRL (Datta et al., 2020a).

## 4 Methods

### 4.1 Sequence Labeling Method (Baseline)

We take a $\text{BERT}_{\text{BASE}}$ model pre-trained on MIMIC (Si et al., 2019) and fine-tune on our annotated corpus to identify the spatial triggers. We treat this as a sequence labeling task where each sentence is WordPiece-tokenized and represented as [[CLS] sentence [SEP]] to construct an input sequence to the BERT encoder as in Devlin et al. (2019). The encoder output is fed into a linear classification layer to predict labels per token. We use the BIO scheme for tagging the spatial triggers.

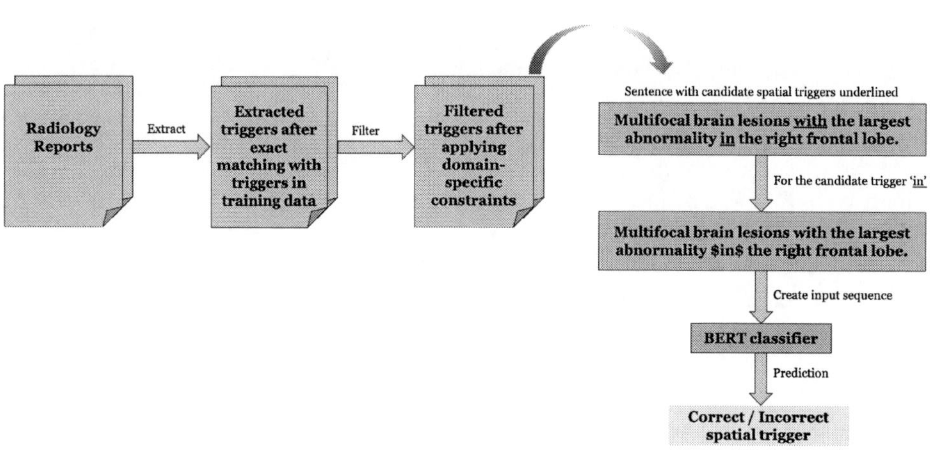


Figure 1: Pipeline of the proposed hybrid approach.

### 4.2 Proposed Hybrid Method

The proposed pipeline is shown in Figure 1.

**Generating candidate spatial triggers** This focuses on extracting spatial triggers in a sentence with high recall. First, we construct a set of all the unique spatial triggers encountered in the training set. Then, we identify the triggers in an unseen radiology report using case-insensitive exact matching against the triggers in the constructed set. In case of the triggers having overlapping spans, we use the longest span as the final candidate trigger. For example, when both the triggers - *extends in* and *in* are identified in a sentence and have overlapping spans, *extends in* is selected as the candidate trigger for the next step.

**Applying radiology-specific constraints** As the candidate generation phase aims to improve recall, this results in the common problem of low precision. Thus we introduce a set of radiology language-specific rules to reduce the number of false positives. We develop the constraints such that they are generalizable across different types of radiology reports. For example, *the left* or *the right* are frequent phrases which are usually followed by the spatial trigger *on*. However, *left* and *right* do not indicate any specific anatomical location. So we exclude *on* from our final candidate trigger list if it occurs in scenarios like this. Thus, for each of the common spatial triggers such as *with*, *in*, and *at*, we develop a set of frequent terms or phrases such that when any of the phrase is seen surrounding a trigger, that particular trigger will be excluded from our final candidate trigger list. Note that we construct separate list of such surrounding phrases

| Spatial trigger | Terms to left | Terms to right |
|---|---|---|
| of | evidence, suggestive, possibility,... | time, position, uncertain, ... |
| with | correlation, compatible, consistent, ... | previous, prior, known, ... |
| to | appear, compared, rotated, ... | suggest, assess, be, ... |

Table 2: Example terms for 3 common spatial triggers.

for left and right side of a spatial trigger. A few examples of the developed phrases are shown in Table 2. The complete list is in appendix Table 4.

**BERT Classifier** A BERT-based classification model is used determine whether each candidate trigger identified in the previous step is correct. We construct the input data as follows:

- Identify the triggers with distinct spans combining both gold triggers and the candidate triggers in a sentence.
- Create a separate sentence instance for each of the triggers obtained from the above step.
- Assign a positive (correct) label to an instance if the associated trigger is a gold trigger and a negative (incorrect) label otherwise.

We construct an input sequence to BERT by converting each of the above instances to the standard BERT input format [[CLS] sentence [SEP]], similar to Section 4.1. Note that the classification of being correct/incorrect is based on a specific spatial trigger in a sentence. In order to inform the model about the positional information of the spatial trigger, we insert a special character sequence '$' both to the left and right of the trigger. The other aspects of the model architecture is similar to the original BERT paper's implementation (Devlin et al., 2019).

## 5 Evaluation and Experimental settings

We perform 10-fold cross validation (CV) to evaluate the performance of both the BERT-based methods. For each of the 10 iterations, reports in 8 folds are used for training and 1 fold each are used for validation and testing. Average precision, recall, and F1 measures are reported for these methods. We also report these performance metric values for the rule-based methods (both for exact matching and exact matching + constraints) by evaluating on the same test folds. Note that we train the BERT classifier using the candidates directly obtained after the exact matching step. While evaluating, we apply the additional domain constraints over the candidate triggers generated from exact matching. We make this decision based on the results of our preliminary experiments.

We use the $\text{BERT}_{\text{BASE}}$ variant for both sequence labeling and classification models. The models are pre-trained on MIMIC-III clinical notes (Si et al., 2019) for 320K steps. The maximum sequence length for both the tasks is set at 128 and learning rate at $2e$-5. Based on the validation set performance, we select the number of training epochs as 4. We use the cased version of the models.

## 6 Results

The results of spatial trigger extraction are shown in Table 3. The average accuracy of the BERT-based classifier model over 10-fold CV is 88.7%.

We notice that the sequence labeling method obtained high precision and low recall. The exact matching achieved a much improved recall (96.77%) compared to the sequence labeling system. However, it resulted in too many false positive spatial triggers, mainly because of common prepositional and verb terms such as *of*, *with*, and *are* (as indicated by a very low precision). We achieved slightly better precision by applying constraints over the exact matched triggers (shown in the third row of Table 3). Our proposed method which utilizes a set of domain-inspired constraints on top of a BERT-based classifier helps in obtaining a balanced precision and recall, improving the F1 by almost 24 points compared to standard BERT sequence labeling.

| Method | P(%) | R(%) | F1 |
|---|---|---|---|
| BERT-Based Sequence Labeling | 92.20 | 43.04 | 57.52 |
| Exact matching | 18.71 | 96.77 | 31.32 |
| Exact matching + Constraints | 34.56 | 93.02 | 50.21 |
| Exact matching + Constraints + BERT-Based Classification | 84.43 | 79.19 | 81.10 |

Table 3: Spatial trigger extraction results. Average Precision (P), Recall (R), and F1 across 10 test folds. 10-fold cross validation is performed for the BERT-based models (first and last rows).

## 7 Discussion

We focus on extracting varied spatial expressions from radiology reports using a sequence labeling method as well as a hybrid approach that first applies domain-specific rules to extract the candidate triggers and later employs a deep learning-based classifier to judge every candidate. Our proposed method (Exact matching + Constraints + BERT-based classification) achieves much improved average F1 measure in CV.

**Error Analysis** We observe that, after applying constraints, most of the triggers that are missed by the rule-based approach are uncommon phrases that are not seen in the training data, e.g., verbs followed by prepositions such as *grows into* and verbs such as *filling*. Whereas, for the proposed hybrid approach, missed triggers are usually verbs such as *demonstrates* and *appears*.

**Challenges** Many of the spatial expressions which describe the presence of an abnormality in a specific anatomical location are common English language terms such as *of*, *with*, and *are*. Some other challenges include identifying whether a 'verb followed by prepositional/adverb' phrase always indicates a spatial expression or not, since in a few cases they imply intermediate change in position (e.g., *kinks back*) rather than the position where a radiological entity is actually located.

**Future Directions** Our next steps include examining the generalizability of our proposed approach when applied to other types of radiology reports (e.g., *ultrasound*, *computed tomography*, etc.). We also aim to incorporate additional rules that can extract spatial expressions beyond the ones seen in the training set. One of the potential rules may be to automatically generate more variations of triggers with the form 'verb followed by preposition'. Using part-of-speech (POS) information to automatically extract triggers holds potential but this may introduce errors from the POS taggers.

## 8 Conclusion

This work proposes a BERT-based hybrid method to extract spatial expressions from radiology reports. This method achieves satisfactory performance with an average F1 measure of 81.10 over 10-fold CV. We also extract spatial expressions by formulating the problem as a sequence labeling task (used as baseline). We find that the BERT-based sequence labeling model suffers from low recall. Our proposed hybrid approach combining radiology-specific constraints with a BERT-based classifier helps to improve the recall by around 36%. We also address some of the challenges involved in the task of spatial trigger extraction in the radiology domain. We plan to further improve the performance of the system by adding more granular domain constraints as well as evaluate the generalizability of the method across multi-institutional datasets.

## Acknowledgments

This work was supported in part by the National Institute of Biomedical Imaging and Bioengineering (NIBIB: R21EB029575) and the Patient-Centered Outcomes Research Institute (PCORI: ME-2018C1-10963).

## References

Muhammad Nabeel Asim, Muhammad Usman Ghani Khan, Muhammad Imran Malik, Andreas Dengel, and Sheraz Ahmed. 2019. A Robust Hybrid Approach for Textual Document Classification.

Surabhi Datta and Kirk Roberts. 2020. A dataset of chest X-ray reports annotated with Spatial Role Labeling annotations. *Data in Brief*, 32:106056.

Surabhi Datta, Yuqi Si, Laritza Rodriguez, Sonya E Shooshan, Dina Demner-Fushman, and Kirk Roberts. 2020a. Understanding spatial language in radiology: Representation framework, annotation, and spatial relation extraction from chest X-ray reports using deep learning. *Journal of Biomedical Informatics*, 108:103473.

Surabhi Datta, Morgan Ulinski, Jordan Godfrey-Stovall, Shekhar Khanpara, Roy F. Riascos-Castaneda, and Kirk Roberts. 2020b. Rad-SpatialNet: A Frame-based Resource for Fine-Grained Spatial Relations in Radiology Reports. In *Proceedings of The 12th Language Resources and Evaluation Conference*, pages 2251–2260.

Jacob Devlin, Ming-Wei Chang, Kenton Lee, and Kristina Toutanova. 2019. BERT: Pre-training of Deep Bidirectional Transformers for Language Understanding. In *Proceedings of the 2019 Conference of the North American Chapter of the Association for Computational Linguistics: Human Language Technologies, Volume 1 (Long and Short Papers)*, pages 4171–4186. Association for Computational Linguistics.

Er. Khushbu Gupta, Ratchainant Thammasudjarit, and Ammarin Thakkinstian. 2019. A Hybrid Engine for Clinical Information Extraction from Radiology Reports. In *2019 16th International Joint Conference on Computer Science and Software Engineering (JCSSE)*, pages 293–297.

Alistair E.W. Johnson, Tom J. Pollard, Lu Shen, Li Wei H. Lehman, Mengling Feng, Mohammad Ghassemi, Benjamin Moody, Peter Szolovits, Leo Anthony Celi, and Roger G. Mark. 2016. MIMIC-III, a freely accessible critical care database. *Scientific Data*, 3:160035.

Xusheng Li, Chengcheng Fu, Ran Zhong, Duo Zhong, Tingting He, and Xingpeng Jiang. 2019. A hybrid deep learning framework for bacterial named entity recognition with domain features. *BMC Bioinformatics*, 20(16):583.

Bryan Rink, Kirk Roberts, Sanda Harabagiu, Richard H Scheuermann, Seth Toomay, Travis Browning, Teresa Bosler, and Ronald Peshock. 2013. Extracting actionable findings of appendicitis from radiology reports using natural language processing. In *AMIA Joint Summits on Translational Science Proceedings*, volume 2013, page 221.

Kirk Roberts, Bryan Rink, Sanda M Harabagiu, Richard H Scheuermann, Seth Toomay, Travis Browning, Teresa Bosler, and Ronald Peshock. 2012. A machine learning approach for identifying anatomical locations of actionable findings in radiology reports. In *AMIA Annual Symposium Proceedings*, volume 2012, pages 779–788.

Yuqi Si, Jingqi Wang, Hua Xu, and Kirk Roberts. 2019. Enhancing clinical concept extraction with contextual embeddings. *Journal of the American Medical Informatics Association*, 26(11):1297–1304.

Xiaosong Wang, Yifan Peng, Le Lu, Zhiyong Lu, Mohammadhadi Bagheri, and Ronald M. Summers. 2017. ChestX-ray8: Hospital-scale chest X-ray database and benchmarks on weakly-supervised classification and localization of common thorax diseases. In *2017 IEEE Conference on Computer Vision and Pattern Recognition (CVPR)*, pages 3462–3471.

## A Appendix

| Spatial trigger | Terms to the left | Terms to the right |
|---|---|---|
| of | mri, mra, mrv, xray, projection, babygram, head, view, history, evidence, suggestive, possibility, evaluation, repositioning, ct, loop, free, level, floor, top, area, circle, suggestion, remainder, shortness, position, component, foci, focus, hour, examination, date, study, reposition, positioning | time, position, normal, certain, uncertain |
| with | made, correlation, brain, xray, ct, mri, mra, mrv, projection, infant, patient, baby, compatible, consistent, catheter, associated | previous, prior, known, exam, lead, port, sideport, wire, its, no, tip, distal |
| to | appear, similar, due, compared, rotated, made, secondary, attributed, related | suggest, assess, be |
| in | increase, decrease, normal, result | size, position, good, satisfactory, appearance, (+ limit as the second or third term to the right) |
| show/demonstrate | mri, mra, mrv, xray, projection, babygram, head, view, history, ct, which | – |
| from | mri, mra, mrv, xray, projection, ct, lead, port, sideport, wire | – |
| on | as, appearance | mri, mra, mrv, xray, projection, ct, chest, brain, head |
| for | evidence, assess | – |
| is/are | there, finding, findings, noted, demonstrated, size, this, nonspecific | normal, stable, clear, maintained, preserved, age-appropriate, unchanged, identified, made, within, recommended, removed, repositioned, replaced, low, high, seen, located, present, absent, unremarkable, remarkable, marked, approximately, noted, no, in, large, larger, small, smaller, otherwise, intact, slightly |
| has been | – | removed, repositioned, replaced, reviewed, resolution |
| within | – | normal |
| has/have | – | increased, decreased, improved |
| above | described | – |
| by | edited, recommended, suggested, reviewed, signed, read | – |
| over | – | to |
| at | – | time mentions (example format–8:18 AM) |
| on/to | – | left, right (second term to the right) |
| all | image, imaging, radiograph, radiography, film, series, comparison is made, time, map (any of these terms to the left of the trigger with window length 3) | image, imaging, radiograph, radiography, film, series, comparison is made, time, map (any of these terms to the right of the trigger with window length 3) |

Table 4: A more exhaustive list of the terms used for building the constraints for a set of spatial triggers in the dataset.

# Retouchdown: Releasing Touchdown on StreetLearn as a Public Resource for Language Grounding Tasks in Street View

**Harsh Mehta**
Google Research
harshm@google.com

**Yoav Artzi**
Cornell University
yoav@cs.cornell.edu

**Jason Baldridge**
Google Research
jridge@google.com

**Eugene Ie**
Google Research
eugeneie@google.com

**Piotr Mirowski**
Deepmind
piotrmirowski@google.com

## Abstract

The Touchdown dataset (Chen et al., 2019) provides instructions by human annotators for navigation through New York City streets and for resolving spatial descriptions at a given location. To enable the wider research community to work effectively with the Touchdown tasks, we are publicly releasing the 29k raw Street View panoramas needed for Touchdown. We follow the process used for the StreetLearn data release (Mirowski et al., 2019) to check panoramas for personally identifiable information and blur them as necessary. These have been added to the StreetLearn dataset and can be obtained via the same process as used previously for StreetLearn. We also provide a reference implementation for both Touchdown tasks: vision and language navigation (VLN) and spatial description resolution (SDR). We compare our model results to those given in Chen et al. (2019) and show that the panoramas we have added to StreetLearn support both Touchdown tasks and can be used effectively for further research and comparison.

## 1 Introduction

Following natural language navigation instructions in visual environments requires addressing multiple challenges in dynamic, continuously changing environments, including language understanding, object recognition, grounding and spatial reasoning. Until recently, the most commonly studied domains were map-based (Thompson et al., 1993) or game-like (Macmahon et al., 2006; Misra et al., 2017, 2018; Hermann et al., 2017; Hill et al., 2017). These environments enabled substantial progress, but the complexity and diversity of the visual input they provide is limited. This greatly simplifies both the language and vision challenges. To address this, recent tasks based on simulated environments include photo-realistic visual input, such as Room-to-Room (R2R; Anderson et al., 2018), Talk-the-Walk (de Vries et al., 2018) and Touchdown (Chen et al., 2019), all of which rely on panorama photos.

A major challenge of creating simulations that use real-world photographs is they at times capture bystanders and their property. This raises privacy concerns and requires additional care to check for and ensure personally identifiable information (PII) is removed from research resources that are made publicly available. Existing resources adopt different strategies to address this. The Matterport3D dataset (Chang et al., 2017), which underlies the R2R task, is focused on real-estate data that is curated to exclude PII. This approach is limited to environments of a specific type: houses that are for sale. Academic resources that focus on urban street scenes opted to manually collect panoramas from scratch and scrub them for PII (de Vries et al., 2018; Weiss et al., 2019). This is laborious and costly—especially the first stage of collecting the panoramas. As a result, such resources cover relatively small areas.

Google Street View has world-wide scale coverage of street scenes. Each panorama in Street View has gone through a process to protect the privacy of bystanders and their property. Individuals can also request specific panoramas to be removed. As such, it is a resource with the potential to transform the research community's ability to study problems such as street scene understanding and navigation. Touchdown relies on 29,641 panoramas from Street View; however, because raw images cannot be distributed according to the Street View terms-of-service,[1] these are not provided with the Touchdown data. Instead, only image feature vectors are available for direct download with the data, and access to the raw panoramas is subject to availability through APIs governed by Street View's terms of service.

[1]https://www.google.com/help/terms_maps/



*Proceedings of the Third International Workshop on Spatial Language Understanding (SpLU 2020)*, pages 56–62
November 19, 2020. 
https://doi.org/10.18653/v1/P17

Research can be done within a company and shared via publication without releasing data; for example, Cirik et al. (2018) discussed models for instruction-conditioned navigation in Street View. However, the full impact of the data and research about it can be better realized by making at least some portion of such resources available to the broader research community. In this context, StreetLearn (Mirowski et al., 2018, 2019) stands out as a publicly available resource of Street View data that has been approved for dissemination and use for academic research.[2] StreetLearn contains 114k panoramas from New York City and Pittsburgh that have been manually checked for PII, ensuring, for example, that faces and license plates are blurred. The dataset can be easily accessed. Researchers interested in working with the data simply fill a form stating their goals and commit to update the data periodically with newer versions as they are released. This process balances the ability of researchers to use the data with preserving the privacy and rights of individuals impacted by the data. For example, periodic updates allow Google to respond to user takedown requests.

To increase the accessibility of Touchdown and provide an example of how important data can be responsibly released, we integrate the Touchdown task and its corresponding Street View data into a new version of StreetLearn. This paper reconciles Touchdown's mode of dissemination with StreetLearn's, which was designed to adhere to the rights of Google and individuals while also simplifying access for researchers and improving reproducibility. We also provide open source implementations[3] of both the vision-and-language navigation and spatial description resolution tasks, which we show to have a consistent performance with the results in the original Touchdown paper. We hope that this release of data and code will enable the entire research community to make further progress on these problems and to consider new questions and tasks enabled by this limited but significant slice of Street View data.

## 2 Process

Touchdown includes tasks for natural language navigation and spatial reasoning in realistic urban environments. Touchdown uses Street View panoramas

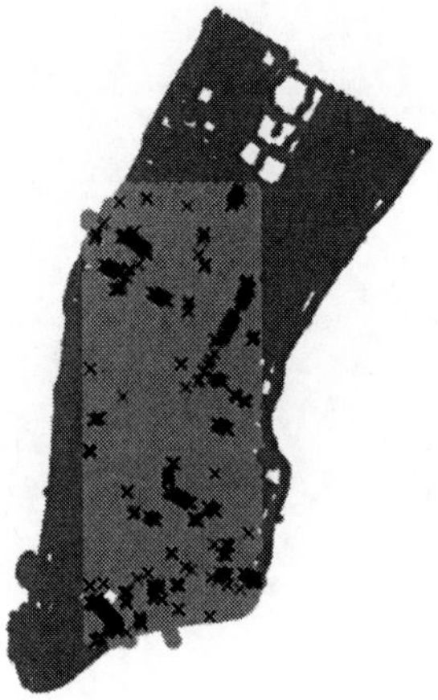

Figure 1: The overlap between the StreetLearn (blue) and Touchdown (red) panoramas in Manhattan. There are 710 panoramas (out of 29k) that share the same ID in both datasets (in black).

of New York City to define a large-scale navigation environment. It includes 9,326 human-written instructions and 27,575 spatial description resolution tasks. Touchdown's instructions were written by people and emphasize attributes of the visual environment as navigational cues. This makes Touchdown a valuable resource for research on following natural language instructions in visual environments. This contrasts with the template-based navigation instructions used by Hermann et al. (2020), which were generated by Google Maps API and used with StreetLearn panoramas.

Unfortunately, the development and release of Touchdown introduced several challenges that complicate working with the data. Even though Touchdown itself does not contain Street View data, it references specific Street View panoramas and depends on access to them via the Street View API. This requires any researcher that wishes to work on the data to download large amounts of data using the API, which is inconvenient, error-prone and not aligned with the current Google Maps terms-of-service. Also, the panoramas available through the API periodically change, potentially making parts of the data unavailable. This means there is no hope for consistent versioning (which hurts reproducibility) regarding panorama availability because the data collected by each researcher is dependent on the particular time they access it. Finally, individual researchers or research groups cannot themselves comply with takedown requests.

[2] http://streetlearn.cc

[3] https://github.com/google-research/valan/tree/master/touchdown

Figure 2: One of the panoramas taken from the dataset which shows transient objects being referenced in the navigation text. *"Stop here, and turn left. You will now be walking down a narrow lane with parked* ***cars*** *on both sides. There should be a payphone on your right and a fire hydrant (behind silver poles) on your left. Walk down this lane, and on your left you will soon see a shop with gray columns between the windows and a blue sign with yellow trim."*

Instead, having the panoramas available as part of StreetLearn allows for necessary updates and consistent sharing of the panoramas.

To address these challenges, we collect, check and release the Touchdown panoramas as part of an update to the 114k existing StreetLearn panoramas, which cover regions of New York City and Pittsburgh. As shown in Figure 1, StreetLearn encompasses the entire region of New York City contained in Touchdown; however, the StreetLearn panoramas themselves are not sufficient for supporting the Touchdown tasks themselves. This is for several reasons.

- The **granularity** of the panorama spacing is different. Figure 1 shows that most of the panoramas are different. Touchdown has roughly 25% of the panos but covers half of Manhattan compared to StreetLearn.

- The language instructions refer to **transient objects** such as cars, bicycles, and couches, as illustrated in Figures 2 and 3. A panorama from a different time period will not contain these objects, so the instructions are not stable across time periods.

- Spatial description resolution requires coverage of multiple points-of-view for those specific panoramas. Figure 3 shows an example SDR description and the corresponding views from which it can be answered.

In all, the Touchdown tasks encompass 29,641 panoramas. All of these went through extensive manual review by annotators to check for personally identifiable information (PII), such as faces and license plates. Regions containing PII were marked as bounding boxes by annotators, and we blurred all of these regions for the final images.

## 3 Experiments

We re-implement the best-reported models on the navigation and spatial description resolution tasks from Chen et al. (2019) to compare performance with our data release to the original Touchdown paper. The key difference between the two settings is that our released panoramas contain additional blurred patches (Section 2). Another minor difference is that we use a word-piece tokenizer (Devlin et al., 2019) instead of a full-word tokenizer.

**Spatial Description Resolution.** SDR results are given in Table 1. Following Chen et al. (2019), we report mean distance error and accuracy with different thresholds (40px, 80px, and 120px), which measures the proportion of evaluation items where the pixel chosen by the model is within the specified pixel distance. Our Retouchdown reimplementation of LINGUNET obtains better performance on the accuracy measures, but worse performance on mean distance error. To check whether this is a consequence of the blurring, we ran our model with features retrieved from original panoramas and obtained similar results as those listed in Table 1. Given this, the performance difference between our model and the original paper are likely not due to the additional blurring. As

Figure 3: Actual example taken from the dataset with multiple SDR panorama viewpoints for the same instruction: *Two parked bicycles, and a discarded couch, all on the left. Walk just past this couch, and stop before you pass another parked bicycle. This bike will be white and red, with a white seat. Touchdown is sitting on top of the bike seat.*

| Method | A@40px ↑ | A@80px ↑ | A@120px ↑ | Dist ↓ |
|---|---|---|---|---|
| *Development* | | | | |
| Chen et al. (2019) | 24.81 | 32.83 | 36.44 | 729 |
| Retouch-LINGUNET | 29.79 | 35.28 | 38.14 | 800 |
| *Test* | | | | |
| Chen et al. (2019) | 26.11 | 34.59 | 37.81 | 708 |
| Retouch-LINGUNET | 30.32 | 36.73 | 39.27 | 793 |

Table 1: SDR development and test results using the LINGUNET architecture, which Chen et al. (2019) reported as the best performing system.

| Method | TC ↑ | SPD ↓ | SED ↑ | NDTW ↑ | SDTW ↑ |
|---|---|---|---|---|---|
| *Development* | | | | | |
| Chen et al. (2019) | 9.8 | 19.1 | 0.094 | | |
| Retouch-RCONCAT | 13.4 | 17.1 | 0.124 | 4.9 | 1.3 |
| *Test* | | | | | |
| Chen et al. (2019) | 10.7 | 19.5 | 0.104 | | |
| Retouch-RCONCAT | 12.8 | 17.1 | 0.131 | 5.0 | 1.4 |

Table 2: Navigation development and test results. We use the RCONCAT architecture, which Chen et al. (2019) reported as the best performing.

such, the Touchdown panoramas available through StreetLearn can be reliably used as direct replacement for those used in Chen et al. (2019).

**Vision-and-Language Navigation.** We use the following metrics to evaluate VLN performance:

- Task Completion (TC): the accuracy of navigating to the correct location. The correct location is defined as the exact goal panorama or one of its neighboring panoramas. This is the equivalent of the success rate metric (SR) used commonly in VLN for R2R.
- Shortest-path distance (SPD): the mean of the distances over all executions of the agent's final panorama position and the goal panorama.
- Success weighted by Edit Distance (SED): normalized graph edit distance between the agent path and true path, with points only awarded for successful paths.
- Normalized Dynamic Time Warping (NDTW): a minimized cumulative distance between the agent path and true path, normalized by path length.
- Success weighted Dynamic Time Warping (SDTW): NDTW, with points awarded only for successful paths.

TC, SPD, and SED are defined in Chen et al. (2019) and NDTW and SDTW are defined in Ilharco et al. (2019).

VLN results are given in Table 2. Our Retouchdown reimplementation of the RCONCAT model improves over the results given in Chen et al. (2019) for all metrics. We also establish benchmark scores for NDTW and SDTW. As with SDR, the panoramas now available via StreetLearn thus do not remove information critical for the VLN task. In our implementation, we use imitation learning on top of a scalable framework based on the Actor-Learner architecture (Lansing et al., 2019), instead of supervised learning using Hogwild! (Recht et al., 2011). These differences likely explain the observed differences with the original results.

Compared to interior navigation in the Room-to-Room (R2R) task, the Touchdown task is much harder: e.g. the current state-of-the-art success rate (equivalent to TC) for R2R on the validation unseen dataset is 55% (Zhu et al., 2019). It is even considerably harder than Room-across-Room dataset, which has longer, more challenging paths than R2R and success rates of 26% to 30% for three different languages (Ku et al., 2020). The same holds for DTW measures: Ilharco et al. (2019) report a success rate of 44% and corresponding SDTW of

38.3% for a fidelity-oriented version of the Reinforced Cross-modal Matching agent (Wang et al., 2019). Ku et al. (2020) reports lower SDTW scores of 21% to 24%. Given this, the TC of 12.8% and SDTW of 1.4% obtained by Retouch-RCONCAT and current best results from Xiang et al. (2020) (TC: 19.0%; SDTW: 16.3%), amply demonstrates the challenge of the outdoor navigation problem defined by Touchdown. The greater diversity of the visual environments and the far greater degrees-of-freedom for navigation thus provide plenty of headroom for future research.

## 4 Conclusion

The research community is interested in using large-scale resources such as Street View for work on computer vision and navigation. In order to comply with Street View's terms-of-service (which allow for only limited use of its data and APIs) and with its data restrictions, we have enriched StreetLearn with panoramas from the Touchdown study. Takedown requests that respect individuals' privacy preferences can be managed through the StreetLearn package. We encourage the research community to use only vetted and approved resources like StreetLearn, including our new release of the Touchdown panoramas, for their Street View oriented work.

The addition of Touchdown to StreetLearn (a.k.a. *Retouchdown*) boosts the total panorama count for the StreetLearn dataset from 114k to 144k. Furthermore, it contains multiple panoramas from the same neighborhoods, which supports work on learning to navigate in a region and testing in that same region using panoramas from a different time. Our code for training and evaluating vision-and-language navigation agents and spatial description resolution models are publicly available as part of the VALAN framework (Lansing et al., 2019).[4]

## References


Peter Anderson, Qi Wu, Damien Teney, Jake Bruce, Mark Johnson, Niko Sünderhauf, Ian Reid, Stephen Gould, and Anton van den Hengel. 2018. Vision-and-language navigation: Interpreting visually-grounded navigation instructions in real environments. In *Proceedings of the IEEE Conference on Computer Vision and Pattern Recognition (CVPR)*.

Angel Chang, Angela Dai, Thomas Funkhouser, Maciej Halber, Matthias Niessner, Manolis Savva, Shuran Song, Andy Zeng, and Yinda Zhang. 2017. Matterport3d: Learning from RGB-D data in indoor environments. *International Conference on 3D Vision (3DV)*.

Howard Chen, Alane Suhr, Dipendra Misra, and Yoav Artzi. 2019. Touchdown: Natural language navigation and spatial reasoning in visual street environments. In *Conference on Computer Vision and Pattern Recognition*.

Volkan Cirik, Yuan Zhang, and Jason Baldridge. 2018. Following formulaic map instructions in a street simulation environment. *NeurIPS Visually Grounded Interaction and Language Workshop*.

Jacob Devlin, Ming-Wei Chang, Kenton Lee, and Kristina Toutanova. 2019. BERT: Pre-training of deep bidirectional transformers for language understanding. In *Proceedings of NAACL-HLT 2019*, pages 4171–4186, Minneapolis, Minnesota. Association for Computational Linguistics.

Karl Moritz Hermann, Felix Hill, Simon Green, Fumin Wang, Ryan Faulkner, Hubert Soyer, David Szepesvari, Wojciech Marian Czarnecki, Max Jaderberg, Denis Teplyashin, Marcus Wainwright, Chris Apps, Demis Hassabis, and Phil Blunsom. 2017. Grounded language learning in a simulated 3d world. *arXiv*.

Karl Moritz Hermann, Mateusz Malinowski, Piotr Mirowski, Andras Banki-Horvath, Keith Anderson, and Raia Hadsell. 2020. Learning to follow directions in street view. Association for the Advancement of Artificial Intelligence (AAAI).

Felix Hill, Karl Moritz Hermann, Phil Blunsom, and Stephen Clark. 2017. Understanding grounded language learning agents. *arXiv*.

Gabriel Ilharco, Vihan Jain, Alexander Ku, Eugene Ie, and Jason Baldridge. 2019. Effective and general evaluation for instruction conditioned navigation using dynamic time warping. *NeurIPS Visually Grounded Interaction and Language Workshop*.

Alexander Ku, Peter Anderson, Roma Patel, Eugene Ie, and Jason Baldridge. 2020. Room-across-room: Multilingual vision-and-language navigation with dense spatiotemporal grounding. In *Proceedings of EMNLP 2020*.

Larry Lansing, Vihan Jain, Harsh Mehta, Haoshuo Huang, and Eugene Ie. 2019. Valan: Vision and language agent navigation.

Matt Macmahon, Brian Stankiewicz, and Benjamin Kuipers. 2006. Walk the talk: Connecting language, knowledge, action in route instructions. In *Proceedings of AAAI*, pages 1475–1482.


[4]`https://github.com/google-research/valan`

Piotr Mirowski, Andras Banki-Horvath, Keith Anderson, Denis Teplyashin, Karl Moritz Hermann, Mateusz Malinowski, Matthew Koichi Grimes, Karen Simonyan, Koray Kavukcuoglu, Andrew Zisserman, and Raia Hadsell. 2019. The streetlearn environment and dataset. *CoRR*, abs/1903.01292.

Piotr Mirowski, Matthew Koichi Grimes, Mateusz Malinowski, Karl Moritz Hermann, Keith Anderson, Denis Teplyashin, Karen Simonyan, Koray Kavukcuoglu, Andrew Zisserman, and Raia Hadsell. 2018. Learning to navigate in cities without a map. *Advances in Neural Information Processing Systems*.

Dipendra Misra, Andrew Bennett, Valts Blukis, Eyvind Niklasson, Max Shatkhin, and Yoav Artzi. 2018. Mapping instructions to actions in 3D environments with visual goal prediction. In *Proceedings of EMNLP 2018*, pages 2667–2678, Brussels, Belgium.

Dipendra Misra, John Langford, and Yoav Artzi. 2017. Mapping instructions and visual observations to actions with reinforcement learning. In *Proceedings of EMNLP 2017*, pages 1004–1015.

Benjamin Recht, Christopher Ré, Stephen J. Wright, and Feng Niu. 2011. Hogwild: A lock-free approach to parallelizing stochastic gradient descent. In *Proceedings of the Conference on Neural Information Processing Systems*.

Henry S. Thompson, Anne Anderson, Ellen Gurman Bard, Gwyneth Doherty-Sneddon, Alison Newlands, and Cathy Sotillo. 1993. The HCRC Map Task corpus: Natural dialogue for speech recognition. In *Proceedings of the Human Language Technology Workshop*.

Harm de Vries, Kurt Shuster, Dhruv Batra, Devi Parikh, Jason Weston, and Douwe Kiela. 2018. Talk the walk: Navigating new york city through grounded dialogue. *CoRR*, abs/1807.03367.

Xin Wang, Qiuyuan Huang, Asli Çelikyilmaz, Jianfeng Gao, Dinghan Shen, Yuan-Fang Wang, William Yang Wang, and Lei Zhang. 2019. Reinforced cross-modal matching and self-supervised imitation learning for vision-language navigation. In *Proceedings of the IEEE Conference on Computer Vision and Pattern Recognition (CVPR)*.

Martin Weiss, Simon Chamorro, Roger Girgis, Margaux Luck, Samira E. Kahou, Joseph P. Cohen, Derek Nowrouzezahrai, Doina Precup, Florian Golemo, and Chris Pal. 2019. Navigation agents for the visually impaired: A sidewalk simulator and experiments. In *Proceedings of the Conference on Robot Learning*.

Jiannan Xiang, Xin Eric Wang, and William Yang Wang. 2020. Learning to stop: A simple yet effective approach to urban vision-language navigation. In *Findings of EMNLP 2020*.

Fengda Zhu, Yi Zhu, Xiaojun Chang, and Xiaodan Liang. 2019. Vision-language navigation with self-supervised auxiliary reasoning tasks.

**Association for Computational Linguistics**
209 N. Eighth Street
Stroudsburg, Pennsylvania 18360

ISBN 978-1-7138-2004-8

9 781713 820048

CURRAN ASSOCIATES INC.
proceedings.com